W9-DFQ-659

Dogs Don't Bite When a Growl Will Do

DOGS DON'T BITE WHEN A GROWL WILL DO

WHAT YOUR DOG CAN TEACH YOU ABOUT LIVING A HAPPY LIFE

MATT WEINSTEIN
and LUKE BARBER

A PERIGEE BOOK

⫿P

A Perigee Book
Published by The Berkley Publishing Group
A division of Penguin Group (USA) Inc.
375 Hudson Street
New York, New York 10014

First edition: November 2003

Library of Congress Cataloging-in-Publication Data

Weinstein, Matt.
    Dogs don't bite when a growl will do : what your dog can teach you about living a happy life / Matt Weinstein and Luke Barber.— 1st ed.
        p.   cm.
    ISBN 0-399-52916-0
    1. Conduct of life.   2. Dogs—Miscellanea.   I. Barber, Luke.
II. Title.

BF637.C5W445 2003
170'.44—dc21

                                                                    2003046017

PRINTED IN THE UNITED STATES OF AMERICA

10   9   8   7   6   5   4   3   2

This book is for Madeline, Celeste, Dopey, Ricky, Schatze, Boston, John, Casey Bear, Sweet Dreams, Katie, Mead, Luna, and Blue—all great teachers, loving companions, and real friends.

We dedicate it also to all those dogs throughout the world that suffer because they live without a human companion to care for them. A portion of the proceeds from the sale of this book will be donated to organizations that are helping them find their way home.

CONTENTS

ACKNOWLEDGMENTS   xi

INTRODUCTION   xvii

1. Dogs Are Happy   1

2. Dogs Show Their Love Openly   5

3. Dogs Love to Play   9

4. Dogs Are Real Friends   13

5. Dogs Know How to Love   17

6. Dogs Aren't Shy About Saying Hello   21

7. Dogs Adapt to Change   25

8. Dogs Take Praise in Stride   31

9. Dogs Listen Deeply (Even If They Don't Understand)   35

10. Dogs Forgive Easily   39

11. Dogs Are Good Company   45

12. Dogs Rejoice in the Small Pleasures   49

13. Dogs Love the One They're With   55

14. Dogs Travel Lightly   59

15. Dogs Bring Joy with Them   63

16. Dogs Keep Hoping   67

17. Dogs Celebrate, Celebrate, Celebrate   71

18. Dogs Ask for Help   75

19. Dogs Don't Bite When a Growl Will Do   79

20. Dogs Take Criticism Without Resentment   83

21. Dogs Don't Mind Being the Butt of a Joke   87

22. Dogs Are Healthy   91

23. Dogs Are Enthusiastic and Energetic   95

24. Dogs Always Come Home   99

25. Dogs, Even Old Ones, Can Learn New Tricks   103

26. Dogs Don't Compare Themselves to Others   109

27. Dogs Don't Need Designer Water—
An Open Toilet Seat Will Do   113

28. Dogs Don't Get Stuck in the Negative   117

29. Dogs Are Easily Entertained   121

30. Dogs Are Happy with a Simple Life   125

31. Dogs Are Patient   129

32. Dogs Know When to Let Go   133

33. Dogs Know How to Get Comfortable   137

34. Dogs Are In Tune with Their Bodies   141

35. Dogs Don't Roll Over for Just Anyone   145

36. Dogs Scratch Where It Itches   149

37. Dogs Are Good Judges of Character   153

38. Dogs Don't Sweat the Small Stuff
(or Anything Else!)   157

Contents

39. Dogs Turn Work Into Play   161

40. Dogs Know How to Receive Gifts   167

41. Dogs Look Beneath the Surface   171

42. Dogs Are Satisfied   175

43. Dogs Don't Care About Dog Breath   179

44. Dogs Are Optimistic   183

45. Dogs Know Their Limits   187

46. Dogs Like Treats   191

47. Dogs Lick Their Problems   195

48. Dogs Know That Every Rear End Has Some Valuable Information   199

49. Dogs Know There Is a Time for Sitting and Staying   203

50. Dogs Don't Complain About the Menu   207

51. Dogs Know the Antidote to Stress   211

52. Dogs Know What They Are   215

53. Dogs Shake Off Their Pests   219

54. Dogs Go with the Flow   223

55. Dogs Are Faithful   227

56. Dogs Run Free   231

57. Dogs Don't Care About Breed   235

58. Dogs Aim to Please   239

59. Dogs Are Loyal   243

60. Dogs Follow Their Noses   247

61. Dogs Are Courageous   251

62. Dogs Are Curious   255

63. Dogs Laugh Freely and Wastefully   261

64. Dogs Are Sensitive   265

65. Dogs Are Compassionate   269

66. Dogs Know When to Hold On   273

67. Dogs Dance with Life and Death   279

   PHOTOGRAPHER CREDITS   283

ACKNOWLEDGMENTS

My old friend, colleague, and mentor, James Hall, said that the acknowledgments page was the most important page in the book. It is a page that invites the authors to see connections and to know that—to rephrase a well-known saying, "It takes a whole village to write a book."

There is not enough space on this page to acknowledge the vast number of people who have supported me in this endeavor. I owe so much to so many. While remembering the entire "village" with deep gratitude, I must at least here mention the following: Lee Paez, my constant and unending source of loving support and encouragement; Steve Mittelstet, John Barrett, Dru Bookout, Jim Irwin, Tom O'Brien, Gary Verett, Bette Somerville, Marje and Dick Takei, Kim and Bryant Williamson, and Ren and Katrina Toppano have all played a part in this work; many of my colleagues at Richland College have helped in a variety of ways; my children Alicia Paez, Kevin Paez, and Rachel Barber continue to inspire, support, and give me hope; our agent Brian DeFiore offered wonderful suggestions early in the process, and this would be a very different book without him; our editor John Duff tolerated my many email inquiries with grace and always offered helpful advice; Carole Valentino was enormously helpful with technical and photography assistance, as were—of course—the photographers themselves (who are listed elsewhere); and, finally, I owe so much to my friend and co-author, Matt Weinstein. As I have said before, there is not a better person with whom to work. Someday we will write us another book.

—L.B.

We thought we were looking for a literary agent, but we got so much more from Brian DeFiore. Brian gave us profound insight into developing the concept for this book—it would not be in its current form without his creative vision of where it was possible to take our original idea.

John Duff, our editor at Perigee, saw the possibilities of this book from the beginning and was incredibly generous and supportive in his comments.

Rick Foster was a one-man support group during the proposal writing phase of this project, generously sharing his insights and expertise as he worked on his own book proposals.

The members of Bernie DeKoven's Deep Fun Internet discussion group contributed a number of chapter titles that we were delighted to be able to use. Our thanks to the group for their ongoing passion for bringing play to the world.

My wife, Geneen Roth, is a brilliant writer and a talented editor, and her merciless editorial comments coupled with her unfailing cheerleading through the difficult times made this book much more than it was.

People always ask me what it was like writing a book with another person. What can I say . . . it was fabulous! My co-author, Luke Barber, was on fire during the writing of this book, and there were so many days when I checked my email first thing in the morning and then found myself dancing around the room in joy after reading his wonderful musings. I look forward to many more such mornings in the years to come.

—M.W.

"If you don't have a dog—at least one—there is not necessarily anything wrong with you, but there may be something wrong with your life."
—Vincent van Gogh

INTRODUCTION

"Never be afraid of the metaphor."

—RAY BRADBURY

There is an old Hasidic story about students who were asked why they sit at the feet of the master. "Is it so that you may hear his great wisdom?" they were asked.

"No," they replied. "We go to see how he ties his shoes."

These students understood that much wisdom could be learned from great teachers by simply observing how they go about their daily lives. In this book you will have an opportunity to observe the way dogs live with their human companions. We invite you to think about dogs in ways that you may not have thought about them before—as teachers who can help you live a more fulfilling, rewarding, and happy life.

There have been many books written about what you can teach your dog, but very few books about what your dog can teach you. *Dogs Don't Bite When a Growl Will Do* is an attempt to turn the tables on the traditional relationship between dogs and their human companions. Ordinarily we call our dogs in an effort to get them to come to us. In this book our dogs call out to us to imagine how we might be able to live a more satisfying, doglike life.

When we suggest that you "live like your dog" it is intended, of course, as a metaphor. Metaphors by their very nature are not to be taken at face value. Often some of the more literal-minded people who we meet ask us in a puzzled voice, "I don't understand. How can I live like my dog? My dog just sleeps all day! What would my boss say if I acted like my dog in the middle of a meeting? My dog just runs to the window and barks at nothing!"

We look our too-literal questioner in the eye and respond, "It's a metaphor! It doesn't mean you have to walk around carrying a stick in your mouth! It's simply a metaphor!"

Just as people don't actually smoke like chimneys or swim like fish, a literal approach to living like your dog could well create severe problems in your life. For example, we don't think that drinking from the toilet bowl is a good idea under any circumstances. Traditional canine greetings in the workplace are bound to bring about a sexual harassment lawsuit. Jumping up on your friends, licking their faces, or humping their legs might have consequences that are—to say the least—undesirable.

Nonetheless, we believe that there is a great deal to be learned from the idea of living like your dog and that the end result will surely lead to a happier life. We are well aware that it is nearly impossible to present a more upbeat, positive, and optimistic image of dogs than you will find in these pages. We are unabashed in our love of dogs, and that shameless love will, no doubt, be obvious in every chapter.

We have written this book in the first person, so this preface is the only place you will encounter the "we" voice. It has been great fun blending our two voices into one, and we have intentionally not disclosed which experiences actually happened to Luke and which happened to Matt. Sometimes it's easy to figure out, and sometimes it's next to impossible. But we're not telling.

As we have written this book, we have laughed, we have

cried, and we have pondered our own lives. In the process, we have fallen even more deeply in love with dogs. We hope you have a similar journey.

Luke Barber   Matt Weinstein
Dallas, TX   Berkeley, CA
January 2003   January 2003

"Dogs are obsessed with being happy."

—JAMES THURBER

DOGS ARE
HAPPY

S how me a dog, and I'll show you a picture of happiness. Think about it. Have you ever heard anyone say of a dog, "Well, he's very successful and lives in a beautiful house, but he's not very happy"?

One reason most dogs are much happier than most people is that dogs aren't affected by external circumstances the way we are. I notice that even when it's pouring rain outside, my dogs, Blue and Celeste, are still excited to go for a walk. As soon as I open the front door to look outside, they're beside me in a flash, standing expectantly, ready for an adventure. I usually wait for a break in the downpour, and then we all dash out together. The fact that the ground is soggy and there are mud puddles dotting the landscape means nothing to the dogs. While I'm gingerly picking my way around the wet spots, the dogs are joyfully splashing right through them. They aren't afraid to get their paws dirty.

Dogs have a wonderful ability to adapt to changes in their environment. Sure, they love to snuggle up on the couch, but if the couch is taken, they're glad to lie down on the floor. Little things like a change in the weather don't seem to affect their happiness at all. The weather is sunny? That's great. It's raining? That's still great. Things don't have to be "just right" for dogs to be happy or to feel good.

Our lives would be better if we realized that it's not the circumstances of our lives that make us happy or unhappy— it's the story we tell ourselves about those circumstances. Our happiness can be independent of whatever "blessings" or "catastrophes" are going on in our lives because happiness is an inner state, not an outer one. Once we realize that fact, then we don't need an excuse to be happy or unhappy. When our friends suspiciously ask us, "What are you so happy about?" we can genuinely respond, "No reason!" Our happiness doesn't need an explanation. We can be happy no matter what is going on.

Of course, my dogs are not happy and playful all the time. They have been known to collapse by the door in a colossal show of disappointment when I leave the house and say, "No! You can't go. You stay here. I'll be back soon." However, their disappointment and discontent evidently passes quite quickly. One time after telling the dogs they had to stay at home, I walked back through the door almost immediately because I had forgotten my car keys. The dogs were already happily playing tug-of-war with a towel they had discovered under the sofa.

Dogs are almost always happy. Unfortunately, the same cannot be said for most people. We humans are in a constant, obsessive search for that "special something" that will make us feel good. We chase after money, possessions, prestige, fame, or the perfect relationship, all in the hope that it will bring us lasting happiness. We are chasing our tails, but for us it is not about play. We discover that the things we run in circles pursuing give us only brief feelings of outer happiness. This outer happiness does not really nurture us or give us what we are truly seeking. Unlike our dogs, whose discontent is fleeting, our happiness is fleeting, and we wonder why.

Happiness is not something that just happens to some people and doesn't happen to others. Happiness is really about making a choice. Being muddy and wet is a good excuse to feel miserable about life. But as my dogs remind me every rainy day, feeling upset is not the only option. It makes just as much sense to say, "I'm all wet and muddy and I'm feeling great!"

Our dogs can be wonderful teachers in showing us the path to happiness. Why be miserable when you can choose to be happy?

"To his dog, every man is Napoleon; hence the constant popularity of dogs."

—ALDOUS HUXLEY

DOGS SHOW THEIR LOVE OPENLY

A headline in the *National Enquirer* reads, HEARTLESS WOMAN TRIES TO TRADE CHILD FOR A CHIHUAHUA. Even though I have verified that this is an actual news item, I still have trouble believing it. First of all, anyone who knows anything about children knows that even the worst child should bring more than a Chihuahua in trade. A halfway decent child should bring at least a small terrier or perhaps even a collie! There is just no accounting for someone who doesn't know the true worth of another human being.

Dogs, you can be sure, do know the value of humans. In fact, my experiences with dogs suggest that they may overvalue the company of their human companions.

Dogs are clearly pack animals, and they value the other members of the pack. They see us, of course, as members of their horde. Without doubt, one of the reasons that my dogs find me so useful is that I have the ability to open cans and retrieve large bowls of dry food from the cupboard. However, their admiration for me clearly goes far beyond my willingness to ensure that they are fed. Otherwise, why would they follow me around the house wherever I go?

No amount of advance explaining will keep them from rising from their comfortable spots on the couch to follow me into my office. "I'm just going to get some stamps!" I tell them. They ignore this useful bit of information, get up anyway, and follow me into my office. In short order, they have made themselves quite comfortable on the rug. Just about the time that they have collapsed into a cozy spot, I find the stamps and head back to the den. With a groan Blue lifts herself from the rug and follows Celeste, who has bounded after me immediately.

Throughout the day we continue this little slow-motion dance—room to room and spot to spot—without much variation. Occasionally, when they are both fast asleep, I can make a clean getaway to the kitchen for a drink of water. However, about the time I turn from the fridge, there they both stand, waiting for me to notice them. "What's up?" their quizzical looks seem to say. "Were you trying to sneak off without us?"

On days when I am cleaning house, our synchronized movements become as ridiculous as they are predictable. The only exception is that they eye me with deep suspicion when I take out the vacuum cleaner. These fearless dogs, who boldly track elk, coyote, porcupine, and skunk in the nearby woods, become shrinking wimps in the face of this whirring electronic monster. The tables are turned for a short while, and they wonder why I am following them from room to room, torturing them. When the vacuuming is completed, we return to our regular room-rotation ritual.

I am quick to admit that I am good company. However, the way my dogs value my comradeship borders on the absurd. The thing is, though—I like it. I like how much they show me that they care about being in my presence. I really appreciate the trouble they put themselves through in order to let me know how important I am to them. It is such a gift to me that they show me their love throughout the day.

I'm not suggesting that we start following those we love from room to room. This sort of stalking behavior may not be the best way to develop healthy relationships. On the other hand, it can never hurt to let the people we care about know how much we value them.

Telling those we love of our love is wonderful, but showing them is even more powerful. I don't think it's possible to do it too often.

*"I do not live to play, but I play in order
that I may live and return with
greater zest to the labors of life."*

—PLATO

DOGS LOVE

TO PLAY

There are very few things that are certain in this lifetime, but here is one of them: I will get tired of throwing the ball long before the dogs are tired of chasing after it. I will be the first one to cry "Uncle!" in a game of tug-of-war with the red cloth snake, the blue octopus, the stretchy brown dachshund, or any of the dog toys at all.

When I pull out the squeaky toy fish, I've never seen one of the dogs give me a look that says, "Can't we do this later? I'm too tired!" Even if the squeaking of the fish has roused them from a sound sleep, the dogs always respond by scrambling instantly to their feet with a look that says, "Great idea! Glad you thought of it! Let's play!"

Dogs have an endless capacity to play. It is definitely one of their top priorities, and they do their best to remind us that it should be one of ours, too.

When I'm working at my desk, the dogs will lie quietly at my side. But after a while, they'll decide that I've worked hard enough. Blue will get up, stretch her body, then shake herself all over. If I still haven't gotten the hint at that point, Celeste will walk over to my chair and begin rubbing her nose against my arm. When I look over to her, she'll cock her head to the side and look up invitingly, as if to say, "Well? Have you had enough work yet? Let's go out and have some fun!"

On these occasions, I walk reluctantly outside and begin to retie my running shoes, and the dogs know that they have won. Celeste grabs a stick in her mouth and begins to run in ever-widening circles around me, increasing her speed with every revolution. Speed is another form of communication for dogs, and the faster she runs, the happier she seems to be. I start laughing out loud to see her big poodle ears flapping in the wind as she dashes by, like miniature wings on the top of her head. Already I'm feeling better, and I haven't even gone ten feet out the door.

I am convinced that Blue and Celeste are on to something important here. I always return to work refreshed from our walk and reinvigorated from our little break. Work and play are connected in that way: I often do my best work after some good play because my head is clear, my body is relaxed, and my spirit is soaring. Taking an occasional break is important in any kind of ongoing work activity, but if the break involves play, it is even more nourishing. If we want to take care of ourselves at work every day, taking a spontaneous play break is the best thing we can do for our health and mental well-being.

As our dogs constantly remind us, anytime is the right time to play.

"His name is not wild dog anymore, but the first friend, because he will be our friend for always and always and always."

—RUDYARD KIPLING

DOGS ARE
REAL FRIENDS

When it comes to friendship, I think it would be exceedingly difficult for my best human friends to compare favorably with my dogs. In fact, I think dogs should be put into some sort of super-friend category.

For many years, when giving presentations about ethics, I have asked the participants to jot down the virtues or traits of character that they most want to see exhibited in their best friends. Invariably traits like loyal, kind, faithful, fun-loving, optimistic, enthusiastic, and trustworthy head the lists. It will probably come as no surprise to you that they have just given a pretty fair description of the family dog.

I know for certain that my dogs are even more accepting of me than those people I consider to be my best friends. I'll wager that if you give it some thought, you will agree.

My best friends, for example, have come to expect gourmet cooking, fine wine, and scrumptious desserts when they come to my house for dinner. I'm pretty sure that they would be ex-friends if I started feeding them out of a can or a sack, and it was the same meal every time. My dogs accept such treatment without a hint of complaint.

Do you think that my human friends would wait in the car for a couple of hours while I take in a movie, work out at the gym, eat in a nice restaurant, or do some shopping? To my dogs, it is a great privilege. They beg to be taken along on these outings.

Suppose I asked my friends to stay in the yard and wait patiently while I go off to work. Or, worse yet, if I asked them to stay in the yard and entertain themselves while I am entertaining other friends. I think not. Do you think my friends would roll over and let me clean their ears with Q-tips and alcohol or bathe them with water straight from the garden hose? What if I started following behind them expectantly with a pooper-scooper?

Let's see, there are so many other things that my friends simply would not allow. I can't imagine them letting me dress them in silly outfits and then pulling them in a wagon for a Fourth of July parade. Or, what if I started telling perfect strangers all about them, including very intimate details about their sex life and their plans to have offspring. Even worse, what if I decided when, where, how often, and with whom they would have sex? For that matter, do you think my friends would let me decide whether or not they should be "fixed"? (I do think that several of my friends would have benefited, however, by turning these decisions over to me.)

I'm sorry, but my friends would rebel if I gave them my finished plate to lick or started scratching them behind the ears primarily because it felt good to me. No, the friendship exhibited by my dogs is in a class all its own. It is so special that "best friend" doesn't quite express the true nature of our relationship.

Occasionally, when someone has done something for a friend that is way beyond the normal call of duty I have heard people remark, "Now, that took a *real* friend!" So, that's the category that I have saved for our dogs. Dogs are our real friends.

"Dogs never lie about love."

—JEFFERY MOUSSAIEFF MASSON

DOGS KNOW HOW
TO LOVE

I read a letter to the editor in *USA Today*, complaining about an article that had mentioned a dog having "unconditional love" for her human companion. The reader was extremely irate that the paper had printed an article that attributed "human attributes to a dog." The writer of the letter went on to explain that dogs are simply driven by basic animal instincts for survival, and if the misguided people who think that dogs actually love them stop feeding their dogs, they will discover soon enough that their dogs have forsaken them.

After reading this, I couldn't decide if the writer knew less about dogs or less about love. I finally concluded that he must not know much about either. In fact, I am certain that if the masses of humans begin to practice as much love as our dogs do, then the world will become a much more loving place.

Over the years I have heard many people make comments about love that show that they think love has little or nothing to do with how someone actually behaves. They say things like, "My husband loves me, but he mistreats me," or "She loves me, but she's off in her own world most of the time." Never once have I heard anyone say anything remotely like, "My dog loves me, but she never shows me any attention." In my house, it is much more likely that you will hear, "Stop showing me so much attention, I've got work to do!"

Many of the greatest spiritual teachers who have graced the face of the earth have tried to get us to understand that love is not about what we say or—for that matter—about how we feel. Their message to us consistently has been that love is about action. Love is about what we do.

These same spiritual teachers have told us how we must act toward our loved ones if we really wish to love them. According to these wise teachers, four of the main actions that make up love are: bringing kindness to those we love; showing compassion to them by acting to remove their suffering; rejoicing when our loved ones are successful; and acting toward them with fairness and justice. If we can do these things, then we are being loving.

It doesn't take a great deal of reflection on these four characteristics of love for me to see that my dogs love me, and that their love is unconditional. My own dogs, of course, are not exceptional in this regard. Virtually every person who has ever shared life with a dog knows the unreserved love of his or her companion. The good news is that we can learn to love each other the way our dogs love us.

For the next week, show your love to those you hold dear as if you were a dog. Run to greet them when they come in the door. Shower them with attention, affection, and kindness (although you may want to draw the line at licking them on the face). If you see that your loved ones are suffering, try to help them by sitting close and snuggling up to them. Let them know that you are there for them. When they are happy or experience even a minor success, rejoice with them. Share your joy about their joy in very demonstrative ways. Finally, treat them with fairness and justice. Let them be who they are, not who you would like for them to be.

If you manage to practice this for a week, then you will have acted with the deep love that dogs provide to us every single day of our lives. I promise that everyone who comes in contact with you during that time will feel blessed. And so will you.

"Q: If you could choose what to come back as,
what would it be?
A: A dog, so my wife would love me more."

—OSCAR DE LA RENTA, INTERVIEWED IN

VANITY FAIR MAGAZINE

DOGS AREN'T SHY

ABOUT SAYING

HELLO

The best way for me to meet new people is to go out walking with my dogs. Blue and Celeste start wagging their tails as soon as a stranger approaches, and they strain at the leash to get even closer as our paths intersect. The dogs are always excited about a chance encounter like this—they never run out of interest in making new friends.

John Steinbeck used this fact to great advantage for himself in his celebrated *Travels with Charley*. As soon as Steinbeck pulled into a trailer camp, he let his standard poodle, Charley, loose to roam around while he made camp. When Steinbeck went looking for Charley some minutes later, he encountered nothing but friendly greetings from people who were excited to meet Charley's human companion. More often than not, Charley's natural friendliness paved the way for a dinner invitation from these strangers.

Dogs have a kind of basic trust that the world is a safe and welcoming place, and the optimistic way they greet strangers reflects that point of view. That's why we humans respond so positively to a dog's friendly greeting. However we rarely greet each other with quite that same degree of friendliness.

After my dogs pull me over to a stranger on the street, and the stranger exclaims about what sweet dogs they are, I offer my hand and introduce myself. The way humans introduce ourselves to each other by exchanging formal handshakes is quite low-key compared to the enthusiastic wiggling and wagging and sniffing that is the way dogs introduce themselves.

Who dreamed up the idea of a handshake, anyway? I've heard a theory that handshakes date back to medieval times, when two people approached each other with open hands to show they weren't carrying any weapons. There's another theory that once you grab someone else's hand it stops him from coming any closer and sets up a protective boundary between the two of you. It certainly is true that we are much more suspicious on first encountering each other than our dogs are.

Once in a great while, I meet someone who uses a handshake to make some genuine, enthusiastic, doglike contact. When I was a young boy, my father's cousin Manny had a wonderful way of greeting me. He would grab my hand to shake it and then keep shaking it for much longer than is customary, all the while rapidly intoning, "Hellomyboysogoodto seeyou. It'sbeensolongyou'relookingwonderful. I'msogladto seeyouagaintoday. . . ." This extended handshake always delighted me, and we both beamed at each other all the while. I always looked forward to his visits.

In a misguided attempt to be friendly, many times people we meet on the street will crouch down and try to shake hands with the dogs as well. "Come on, give me your paw!" they'll say. The dogs sniff the outstretched hand, look this person up and down with puzzled expressions on their faces, and then look back at me as if to say, "Do I have to shake his hand?"

I'm as guilty as most everyone else about teaching my dogs to shake hands. However, it seems clear to me that my dogs view shaking hands as a little performance rather than a greeting. Dogs already greet new friends so passionately they don't need lessons from us in how to make contact. Instead, we could take lessons from them. If we could learn to greet the people we meet with the same basic trust, openness, energy, and enthusiasm that is second nature to our dogs, the world would be a much friendlier place.

*"I wonder if other dogs think poodles are
members of a weird religious cult."*

—Rita Rudner

Dogs Adapt to

Change

For most of my life, I wouldn't have been caught dead around poodles. Growing up, my dog heroes were Lassie and Rin Tin Tin. They were the kind of dogs that every boy I knew wanted—big, strong, loyal, intelligent, and loving. I never ended up with either a collie or a German shepherd, but I never lost the desire for those qualities in my dog friends. Once I found out about golden retrievers I was hooked—I was a golden retriever guy. In fact, not long ago I took a canine personality test and discovered that I *am* a golden retriever!

Although I am particularly partial to golden retrievers, I am at heart simply a dog person. I love them all. However, there were always some kinds of dogs that I could never imagine hanging around with. Chief among these was the poodle. I just couldn't picture myself as the poodle type. Life, of course, has a way of handing us things that we don't expect. One of the last things I could have imagined was that I would soon be living with a year-old standard poodle—and worse yet, a poodle named Sweet Dreams.

Sweet Dreams lived with one of my dearest friends. Sharon was diagnosed with a brain tumor shortly after she got Sweet Dreams, and the dog became her closest companion during the last year of her life. The two of them were inseparable. When my friend died, she left Sweet Dreams to my wife and me in her will.

My wife, in her ever-so-positive way, reassured me, "She's a great dog. You will grow to love her in no time, just like our golden." "But . . . but . . . she's a poodle!" I protested, as if that explained everything.

Sweet Dreams came along with several nicknames. One was "*Tout de Suite*," which seemed fitting, given her French heritage. I assumed the nickname came from her ability to come "right away" when she was called. But I was wrong. It was actually derived from her disgusting habit of passing enormous and audible blasts of noxious French poodle gas after every meal.

I was not amused. My wife had a good laugh at my expense when she "reassured" me further, "I've heard that poodles live for sixteen or even eighteen years!"

I could not imagine the next fifteen years of my life spent with this big, curly, delicate, farting dog. I soon went through all of the well-known Kubler-Ross stages of grief and loss, and not just because I had lost my dear friend. I had also gained a poodle!

First, there was the stage of denial and isolation. When we took the dogs for a walk, I used several techniques. I always made my wife walk with Sweet Dreams. I tried to run ahead with our golden retriever and pretend that I didn't know them. When I was caught in a situation where it was clear that I was with them or—horrors—on those few occasions that I had to walk Sweet Dreams by myself, my response was the same. "She's my wife's dog."

Next, came anger. My hostility came out in a variety of ways, including trying to change her name. "I'm going to call her 'Whoopie' from now on," I announced.

"Why would you do that?" was my wife's quick response. "She knows her name already. It would just confuse and upset her."

"Because she is black and very funny," I replied without smiling.

"Come on, let's go, Sweetie," my wife called out to the dog. "Somebody needs to take a time-out in his room!"

By the time two more months had passed, I was heavily into the bargaining phase. Sweet Dreams's hair was beginning to get very, very long, and my wife started to lobby for a poodle cut. I, on the other hand, thought her long hair was a great disguise. Now, when I took her out people would remark, "That's a very unusual dog. What breed is she?"

My standard response was, "She's an English retriever!"

The best part was that it was working. With her new hairstyle, people didn't even know she was a poodle. So I bargained with my wife, "We can keep her . . . as long as we don't cut her hair."

The depression stage set in when I was immediately overruled and my wife took Sweet Dreams to the groomer. Sweetie was clearly as happy about the situation as I was depressed. She danced and pranced around with enormous delight about her new coiffure. Her whole being seemed to shout, "I am poodle, hear me roar!"

She noticed quickly, however, that I was not happy. She walked over to where I was sitting and placed her freshly cut chin on my leg. She rolled her dark eyes upward and looked me square in the eye. Her face said, "I'm not sure why you are so sad, but I'm here for you." One look from those soft eyes and I was ready for the final stage . . . acceptance.

For the next fourteen years, Sweet Dreams was my loyal, loving companion. Whenever I was feeling bad, she had that same way of standing next to me and putting her chin on my leg. She was always there for me. Sweet Dreams was, in fact, the first of my dogs to help me see dogs as wise teachers of the good life. One of the most important lessons she taught me was about accepting and adapting to change. During those early months, while I was having such difficulty accepting her for who and what she was, she had no such difficulty whatsoever accepting me. I now realize it was she, in those early months, who was facing the greater challenge.

Sweet Dreams, in her short time on earth, already had been faced with many changes in her life. She lost her best friend to cancer. She was adopted into a strange new family that included both other dogs and a man who was irrationally prejudiced against poodles. She adapted to each change with the same grace, dignity, and beauty that characterized her every step.

My wife was out of town the day that Sweet Dreams died. In my sadness over the loss of my great friend, Sweetie,

I remember saying to her on the telephone, "Someday, we will find us another poodle."

Indeed, that has come to pass. We have another poodle now, a big, beautiful apricot standard named Celeste. We can all learn to change.

"The dog has seldom been successful in pulling man up to its level of sagacity, but man has frequently dragged a dog down to his."

—JAMES THURBER

DOGS TAKE PRAISE
IN STRIDE

When Celeste goes for a walk down the street with me, rhinestones on her collar and bows in her hair, total strangers stop what they are doing to walk over and talk to her. "What a beautiful girl you are!" they tell her and, "What a good dog you are!" Then they turn to me and ask questions about Celeste, wanting to know how old and what breed she is. They want to know all about my dog but are completely uninterested, it seems, in finding out anything about me. No one has ever said to me the kind of things they say to Celeste, like, "What a beautiful man you are!" and "What a good person you must be!"

Dogs seem to thrive on compliments, but our culture has taught us to feel shy about giving compliments to each other and embarrassed about receiving too much praise. For us humans, receiving compliments is like playing a rapid-fire game of verbal tennis, in which the object of the game is to keep the ball off our side of the court. First, a colleague at work rifles a big serve in my direction, saying, "You did a really good job today!"

I immediately respond with a deflection, slamming a cross-court forehand return, "Oh, I couldn't have done it without you!"

He is undeterred, and tries to sneak a backhand lob right by me, "No, you were just great. I really admire the way you handled everything. I'm really learning a lot from you."

It's time for me to escalate my defense and put an end to this before it gets really embarrassing. I move right into denial, rush the net, and slam an overhead winner right by him, "To tell you the truth, anybody could have done what I did. I didn't really know what I was doing. . . . I got lucky, that's all. In fact, I'm lucky they don't fire my butt right out of this job!" Game, set, match.

Most of us will go to great lengths to shut down excessive

praise before it gets too embarrassing. A few years after I had graduated from college, I was eating dinner in a restaurant in midtown Manhattan, and my favorite professor from my undergraduate days came walking in the door and sat down at a table by himself. I had become much more open about expressing my emotions after I had left school, so I decided to walk over and tell him all the things I had been too shy to let him know when I was his student. I started showering him with compliments, told him how much I had enjoyed his classes and what an inspiration he had been to me. I told him how I would wake up in the predawn hours to get to his early-morning class, and how I wouldn't have done that for anyone else. I told him that I still remembered many of his lectures after all those many years.

At first he started smiling, and I could see he was glad to hear from me, but very shortly the praise started getting too much for him to hear. He began glancing around, doing anything he could to avoid meeting my eyes. He slumped down in his chair and waved his hands feebly in front of him, murmuring softly, "No, no" in an attempt to fend me off. I could see the whole thing was making him incredibly uncomfortable, and finally, in desperation, he lifted the menu up in front of his face and hid behind it. I finally got the message, and backed off. "Well, great to see you again!" I said cheerily, and walked back to my table, wondering whether I had done more harm than good.

The two words Celeste hears most often in her life are, *Good Dog!* I constantly praise her for every little thing she does, and I can tell she enjoys the kind words. She cocks her head to one side, the better to listen to what I have to say, and wags her tail vigorously to show her appreciation. She lets her tongue loll about as if to say, "I am lapping up all this positive attention!"

How wonderful it would be if I could simply say, "Good Professor!" to my old teacher and have him receive it with that same kind of joy.

"No one appreciates the very special genius of your conversation as the dog does."

—CHRISTOPHER MORLEY

DOGS LISTEN DEEPLY (EVEN IF THEY DON'T UNDERSTAND)

Our dogs' capacity for listening is one of the most appealing things about them. The way our dogs cock their heads to the side and stare at us with deep concentration as they hang on our every word is enough to make them friends for life. One of the reasons that we appreciate the quality of deep listening in our dogs is that we don't get enough of it from other people. We all know that being listened to is one of the greatest gifts we can receive, but one that doesn't happen very often.

Nikie, a 120-pound golden retriever, was the only therapy dog certified to work at the World Trade Center site during the massive rescue efforts. Nikie listened to hundreds of construction workers, police officers, and rescue workers talk about the stress of working at Ground Zero. Nikie always listened patiently as the suffering humans talked about everything from broken marriages to childhood memories. One man who worked in the morgue reportedly talked to Nikie for almost an hour after a difficult day on which many remains were found.

Several rescue workers said that it was nice to talk to people, but talking with Nikie was really different. They knew that they could say whatever they were thinking and feeling to a dog and knew that they would be heard without judgment or the need to "fix" their problems.

Nikie's handler and human companion, Frank Shane, said that after long, twelve-hour days at Ground Zero, it was necessary to help Nikie cope with his own stress and tension. Each night after work, Mr. Shane would give Nikie a relaxing massage. For the first few months Nikie worked at the location, he experienced fitful dreams and howled in his sleep. According to Mr. Shane, Nikie not only absorbed the stress of others, "he had to release it."

Few of us will ever have to work or live in an emotionally

charged environment like Nikie's, but the art of deep listening is essential for everyday living as well. Deep listening is not simply hearing. Deep listening involves listening with all our attention, so that we may come to understand the other person. It doesn't necessarily mean that we will try to help with their problem beyond giving our ear and our heart. It certainly does not involve listening so that we can disagree with or contradict the other person.

There has been a great deal written recently about the different ways men and women view the world, including the way that men and women listen to each other. Traditionally, men have a tendency to listen too much in terms of propositions. By definition, propositions are either true or false, and they refer to some state of affairs in the universe.

For example, if my wife says to me, "You never take out the garbage," I hear this as a proposition. I immediately begin to search my mind to see if the proposition actually reflects a state of affairs in the universe. I think to myself, "Let's see. I remember taking the garbage out just last month!" Clearly, this is an indication that my wife's proposition is in error, and I respond accordingly, "That's just false!"

If I were listening deeply, then I might hear what is being said beneath the actual words. I might hear those things that are being left unsaid: that my wife is feeling overwhelmed; that she needs my support. And, if by my deep listening I could hear those things, then I would be much more able to respond out of love rather than defensiveness.

Deep listening involves listening with compassion, so that by our listening alone we help to alleviate suffering in other people. It involves listening without prejudice or judgment. And it involves listening so deeply that we are aware not only of what is said but also what is left unsaid.

I just realized I have a few things I need to get off my chest about how I feel about all this. "Blue! Celeste! Come over here!"

"I've seen the look in dog's eyes, a quickly vanishing look of amazed contempt, and I am convinced that dogs think humans are nuts."

—JOHN STEINBECK

DOGS FORGIVE
EASILY

I remember well the evening of Blue's first birthday party. My wife and I had prepared a cat-food concoction to serve to the dogs. Like so many of us, dogs love to feast on those foods that are most forbidden. So, we always serve our dogs cat food on special occasions. It is as if you can see their eyes light up, "Feline Food Fiesta!"

At this particular time we had three dogs, and Blue, the birthday girl, happened to wander too close to the cat food treat of Casey Bear. Casey was the kindest of dogs, a big, loving golden retriever who would not—under normal conditions—even growl at another being. She was the least dominant of all our dogs. However, this was different. This was cat food!

In a flash, she ferociously attacked Blue, and before we knew what was happening, all three dogs were locked into what seemed like a fight to the death. Before cooler heads prevailed, Blue had a deep gash in her eye socket, and her bloodshot eye looked as if it might fall out. We were into parents' full-panic mode, grabbing for ice and other first-aid treatments, when we noticed that all three dogs had already made peace. All three were wagging tails and kissing each other. Casey Bear was licking Blue's new wound, and Blue was enjoying being comforted by her sisters. It was over. No one was holding a grudge.

Dogs forgive easily, but many of us know people who have held on to grudges for decades. Until recently, I was one of those people.

In my college community lived a colleague whom I shall call "Professor Minefield." He and I were as different as two people could be. For example, I was actively involved in the development of a Peace Studies program on campus. Professor Minefield was the faculty sponsor for the War Games Club. I very much preferred to teach small classes, where I could sit in a circle with my students and develop more direct relationships. Professor Minefield once remarked that if it were up to him he "would lecture in a football stadium." He didn't really mind how many students sat in on his lectures because he didn't plan to let them ask questions anyway.

In reality, we didn't know each other very well. Most of our information about each other was derived through gossip and hearsay. After some disagreement that was so insignificant that it is now lost to memory, Professor Minefield and I worked side-by-side on the same campus for the next twenty years, refusing to speak to one another.

I remember once when a student visiting me in my office remarked that Professor Minefield and I were her "two favorite professors." Rather than being able to accept her very nice compliment, I was upset. *How,* I thought, *could this be possible?* Instead of thanking the student for her confidence in me, I wanted to argue with her. I said, "You must be a little schizophrenic!" I refused to believe anything positive about my hated colleague.

Walking through the Campus Center one day, I saw Professor Minefield in animated conversation with two men in military uniform. He literally had his arms around the shoulders of these men who, I assumed, were military recruiters working on campus. At that moment, I realized that in twenty years of hating Professor Minefield I had only managed to make myself miserable. I certainly had not managed, through my behavior, to change him at all. So, I decided to try to achieve the wisdom of my dogs. I decided to see him as a potential playmate. I decided that I would try to love him instead of hate him.

For the first time in twenty years, I spoke directly to Professor Minefield as I walked by. "Good Afternoon, Professor Minefield! You look like you are right in your element." (Admittedly, I was not yet all the way to love. These were the first, unsure baby steps in the direction away from despising him.) Professor Minefield seemed somewhat taken aback. He didn't speak to me directly, but as I walked past he mumbled something to his new friends about "liberals."

I stopped and took a few steps back toward the group and said, "Professor Minefield, you don't think I'm a liberal do you?"

He appeared surprised and a little uncomfortable that we were actually having a conversation. He said, "You are too a liberal. You're the worst of the whole lot on campus!"

Staying calm I responded, "No, I'm not a liberal. I don't even like liberals!"

He now had a very surprised look on his face. He said, "REALLY?"

With a very straight face I said, "Really. I'm not a liberal, I'm a radical!" Then I broke into a huge smile.

Professor Minefield seemed to like the idea of me not being a liberal, and he started to laugh.

From that day forward we have never passed each other on campus without exchanging a few words. I'm not suggesting that either of us has changed much about what we believe. I am suggesting, however, that in that moment we were transformed from being enemies into being playmates. Just how far we have come was made clear to me not long ago.

I once heard the Zen master, Thich Nhat Hanh, say that the most wonderful thing that we can do in life is to find peace and then share it with another person. Upon hearing this I decided that—from that day forward—I would sign the end of all my communications with the salutation, "Peace." So, all of my letters, email messages, notes, etc., are signed, "Peace."

As an officer in the Faculty Association, one of my duties was to notify those faculty members who had not yet paid their annual dues. So, I wrote a note of reminder and then photocopied it to send to the twenty or so faculty who had not yet paid. Naturally, it ended with my standard, "Peace." I slipped the notes into the appropriate faculty boxes and never gave it a thought when I slipped one of the notes into the box of Professor Minefield.

The next day I received a note with a dues check attached from Professor Minefield. His note read, "Thanks for the reminder. Attached please find a check for my annual dues." At the bottom he had signed, "Peace . . . through military readiness and first-strike nuclear capabilities!"

I laughed so hard that tears came into my eyes. Our political and personal differences might be profound; however, now we were playmates.

After twenty wasted years, our grudge match had finally ended.

LESSON 11

"Whenever you hear that someone else has been successful, rejoice. Always practice rejoicing for others—whether your friend or your enemy. If you cannot practice rejoicing, no matter how long you live, you will not be happy."

—LAMA ZOPA RINPOCHE

DOGS ARE GOOD COMPANY

When I wake up in the middle of the night with a burning idea for some new project, I quietly sneak out of the bedroom, so I won't awaken my wife. I head for the study, where I turn on my computer. After a few minutes, when they're certain I'm not coming back to bed, the dogs rouse themselves from their dog beds and follow me into the study. They shake themselves all over to wake up more quickly, and then they look up at me expectantly. "Okay, what's happening? Where's the action?"

When it's clear that there is no action, they make themselves comfortable on the floor and return to a kind of half-sleep. They don't care what I'm doing—they just want to be close to me. It's a very comforting feeling for me to have them by my side in the early hours of the morning. Even in their semisleeping state, I know that a part of them is always aware of what I'm doing and monitoring my actions. As soon as I turn off my reading light, before I've even finished shutting down my computer, they're instantly awake and on their feet, ready to head out the front door for a walk. Whatever I want to do, on whatever schedule, that's fine with them. They just want to be included.

My dogs are happy to match their moods to mine. Whenever I get an exciting phone call, the dogs get excited, too. As my voice gets louder and more enthusiastic, the dogs can't sit still. They run around in circles and start barking their own excitement. They don't have to understand the subject matter. If I'm happy, then they're happy. If I'm excited, they're excited. Dogs are always good company in that way.

Buddhist teachers have a word for this quality, *Mudita*, which means, "Joy in the joy of others." Whenever I first meet a new person, I'm very sensitive about the direction our conversation is taking. I can talk as passionately about my life and work as the next person, but I like to be invited to do so before I launch into my spiel. But sometimes I find that people I meet can't stop talking about themselves long enough to find out who I am, much less take joy in my joy. I find the old joke, "But enough about me—what do you think of me?" to be all too true in real life.

I was once part of an illuminating team-building experiment, where the members of our organization were randomly divided up into work groups of six people. Each team was given a raw egg, some plastic straws, and some masking tape, and told that our job was to "design a delivery system" out of the materials so that when the egg was dropped from a height of ten feet, it wouldn't break. During the design phase my team wasted so much time trying to figure out how to create shock absorbers out of the plastic straws that we almost didn't complete the project on time. When time had expired, the facilitator asked us to look around the room at each other's designs. We were all amazed at how many different contraptions had been built out of the same raw materials.

Next it was time to begin the "crash tests." The first vehicle to be launched looked fairly secure, with the payload all wrapped up in masking tape, so that you couldn't even see the egg inside. However, the *splat* it gave upon hitting the ground was unmistakably that of an egg cracking, and the disappointed groans of its designers were drowned out by the laughter and applause of the rest of us.

As the facilitator climbed his stepladder and held out the next egg, poised for its maiden flight through space, he asked all of us an interesting question. "Those of you who are not on the team that built this device, I want you to look inside yourself right now and notice if you are hoping that this team will succeed or fail. And if you are rooting for this team to fail, take a moment to ask yourself why. . . ."

In the discussion that followed, most of us were honest enough to admit that we were, in fact, hoping for the other teams to fail. We were all working under the unconscious assumption that the worse the other teams did, the better our team would do. Yet, as the facilitator pointed out to us, this was not a "win or lose" experience: There was room for everyone to win. He reminded us that one person's success in an organization can open up new opportunities for everyone else. Instead of just looking out for our own "team" or "department," we could see ourselves as part of a larger team that encompassed the entire organization.

Life is not a "win or lose" experience, either. Someone else doesn't have to lose for us to win. In our everyday lives, all of us are part of a larger team than just our own family unit—we are all human beings. We can all sense inside of ourselves a deep and profound connection to the rest of humanity and to all other living beings. When we are in touch with that larger vision of our true place in the nature of things, it's easy to be interested in everyone and everything we meet.

Once you can take joy in the joy of others, you will be welcome company wherever your travels may take you.

"To sit with a dog on a hillside on a glorious afternoon is to be back in Eden, where doing nothing was not boring—it was peace."
—MILAN KUNDERA

DOGS REJOICE

IN THE SMALL

PLEASURES

I first fell in love with a dog when I was six years old. My dad brought home a tangled mess of a stray cocker spaniel that he had found wandering aimlessly along the highway. I was instantly smitten—and this was even before I discovered that this was the smartest dog who had ever lived. Dirty and matted as he was, this little cocker would sit, stay, and roll over at my command the first night that he came to live with us. The next day I discovered that he could very cleverly let himself in and out of the screen door whenever he wished. The only smart thing that he would never do was answer to the name that I decided suited him perfectly, "Smarty."

My eleven-year-old sister, who cared nothing for the dog, loved to make my life miserable. So she decided to torment me by renaming the dog "Dopey." How a smart dog like that could ever fall for my sister's ruthless trickery is a mystery to this day. We had a week of dog-calling contests in which my pleas to "Smarty" were totally rejected and my sister's calls of "Come here, Dopey!" were greeted with a vigorous stubby-tailed wagging that evoked laughter from my entire family. Eventually I gave up, and "Dopey" he became.

I have never had a dog that didn't appreciate life's small pleasures. I don't think, however, that I have ever had a canine companion that ever was more demonstrative in showing just how much he loved the little joys in his life than Dopey. Dopey loved having his stomach rubbed so much that he would come trotting up to me and fall over to expose his ready belly. I always stopped whatever I was doing to give him a gentle rub. His tongue would gently loll out of one side of his smiling mouth as his eyes took on the glazed, far-off look of one who is totally lost in a state of ecstasy.

I believe the thing that makes dogs such connoisseurs of the simple pleasures in life is that they give them their full attention. When I scratch my dogs behind the ears, they are in paradise. I don't think they are wondering about world problems or worrying about what they should do next. They are fully present for the joy of having their ears scratched. The good news is that the small pleasures that life has to offer us are not only abundantly available, but are also usually free. The problem is that we are so caught up in pursuing the Big Pleasures that we let the small pleasures slip by. Giving our attention to the little pleasures in life is a difficult thing when we are always busy doing other things.

We have such great expectations about the Big Pleasures in life that when we finally get the chance to experience one, we are often left with the feeling, "Is that all there is?" We convince ourselves that there will be such great pleasure for us when we get that hefty raise, the new car, or that long-awaited vacation. Yet, when we hock the small pleasures available in each and every moment in exchange for the dream of some distant, future pleasures, we end up missing most of our lives.

When we focus more of our attention on the small pleasures in life, then life itself can become a Big Pleasure. For example, few pleasures in life can compare to watching the trees sway in the morning breeze—if we take the time to notice. Those kinds of small pleasures are everywhere if we pay attention.

There is a classic Zen story about a monk who returned to his hut late one evening and discovered a thief stealing his scanty possessions. As the thief was running away, the monk said, "Wait! Please take my robe, as well." When the surprised thief ran off into the night, the monk took a seat on the ground and began to contemplate the pleasures of the night sky. With a peaceful smile upon his face he said wistfully, "I wish I could give him this breeze. I wish I could give him this moon."

The breeze, the moon, and so many other joyful, nourishing pleasures are available to us every day. No matter what else is going on in our lives, we always have the option of taking a few moments and giving our full attention to the small pleasures. These pleasures are always waiting for those of us who are not too dopey.

"Nobody can fully understand love unless he's owned by a dog."

—GENE HILL

DOGS LOVE THE ONE THEY'RE WITH

If you're traveling in Maui and in need of a little doggie love, stop by the Maui Town Market. The proprietor, Chris Borges, will let you take one of her eleven dogs for the day. For free. There's no charge at all for this service.

"I know people when they're on vacation must miss their dogs, so I let them use my dogs," Ms. Borges told the *New York Times*. But it's a win-win arrangement, because the tourists "help me exercise them. It's hard to exercise eleven dogs." Every day the dogs excitedly jump into cars with complete strangers for their day-long adventure. Chris Borges reports that she has never lost a dog, and as far as she knows, her dogs have never had a bad experience.

Dogs know that there's always plenty of love to go around. They are not stingy with their love. In fact, dogs seem to know that the opportunities to experience love are limitless. It's not that only a few people are worthy of our love. Love is everywhere because we always carry our love inside us. It's only when we make the mistake of thinking that love is located outside of us, when we assume that love is dependent on being around a certain person or a certain set of circumstances, that love seems hard to find.

When my wife and I go out of town, Celeste sometimes stays with her brother Sam and his family. As I drive up the street to Sam's house, Celeste starts barking enthusiastically. As soon as I open the car door, she leaps out of the car and bounds over to the front gate, and she and Sam run around wildly on opposite sides of the fence, barking impatiently. When I begin to unlatch the gate, Celeste forces her way through, and she and Sam chase each other merrily around the yard. When Sam's human companions come to the front door, Celeste rushes over to greet them, wagging her tail and snuggling up against them with delight. I can see why they like having her around.

I say my good-byes, and Celeste hardly notices my departure. I try not to take it personally. After all, I don't want to see her moping around, just so I can prove to myself that she loves me! I'd much rather she'd be happy when I'm not around, and I intend to have a happy day without her around, too!

When I return to pick her up the following evening, Celeste, Sam, and his human family are all snuggled on the bed together, watching a video. As I enter the room Celeste lifts her head invitingly and wags her tail rapidly, as if to say, "Come on and join us! We're having a great time over here!"

Dogs know that love is not a precious jewel that needs to be hoarded and only taken out on special occasions. Love is everywhere. It's not hard to find. You take it with you wherever you go.

*"Don't carry anything that's too big
to fit in your mouth."*

—CONVERSATIONS WITH DOG

DOGS TRAVEL
LIGHTLY

When Celeste was a puppy and I began taking her for long walks, she would constantly search around for something to carry in her mouth as we explored the country-side together. She would locate a stick or a pinecone and prance alongside me displaying it quite proudly. I thought it was completely adorable.

Then one day she discovered the mounds of dried horse poop on the trail. She would spot a huge pile of horse drop-pings ahead of us, sprint ahead, and by the time I caught up with her she would be proudly carrying an oversized horse chip in her mouth. None of my pleadings could get her to drop her repulsive trophy, and for obvious reasons I was too disgusted by the whole thing to try to pry it out of her mouth with my hands.

Fortunately the novelty wore off after a few months, and Celeste once again returned to her sticks and pinecones. One thing that impresses me about the way Celeste related to these objects that she carried was that when she was finished with them, she just dropped them and left them there on the trail. She didn't take them home and store them away and hoard them for possible future use. When they had outlived their usefulness, she returned them to the trail, and moved on to the next thing. Dogs occasionally get attached to a special toy or blanket, but they don't get caught up in having lots of possessions the way we do. They don't let the things they're attracted to bog them down. They travel lightly through life.

Most people I know love to be surrounded by their posses-sions. We feel secure when we have more things with us than we need at any given moment. But the problem is that the more possessions we bring along with us, the more time and energy we need to exert making sure we don't lose what we already have. We drag our ever-expanding suitcases behind us throughout the journey of our lives, and then we complain that we can't move as fast as we used to, we're too weighted down with responsibilities, and we don't feel quite so free anymore.

When my friend Ellen Friedman went to Italy on a two-week vacation, she was distraught to discover that the airline had lost her baggage. Because she was constantly traveling from town to town, it took ten days for her luggage to catch up with her. She was amazed to find that she did just fine during that time. "I never would have believed I could have gotten by with such a tiny amount of stuff," she said afterward. "If somebody had said to me, 'you can only go on this trip if you take this tiny little bag,' I probably would have stayed home! When my luggage finally arrived, I asked myself, 'What was I thinking when I packed all this stuff? What do I need all these clothes for?' It was actually a great adventure having to fend for myself like that. It was like I had become an entirely different person in those ten days without my things!"

It can be a liberating experience to free oneself from worrying about one's possessions. Of course this same thing is true of what is called "emotional baggage" as well. When we constantly think about the past, when we spend time worrying about our difficulties with other people and the injustices that were done to us, then our ability to live lightly and joyfully in the present is greatly compromised. Our lives will be so much happier if we can practice leaving more of our emotional and material baggage behind.

I was reading recently about the ancient Stoic philosopher Diogenes who thought that possessions were such a burden in life that he had reduced his belongings to nothing but a simple drinking cup. Then one day he had a flash of insight when he saw a young boy drinking from a stream. "I don't need this cup. I can drink from the palm of my hand!" So, he flung the cup away.

I remember thinking that had my dogs met this old philosopher they might have said, "What? So you think you need hands for drinking?"

LESSON 15

"Make the best use of what is in your power, and take the rest as it happens."

—EPICTETUS

DOGS BRING JOY
WITH THEM

I found myself floating facedown in the Rogue River, hanging on desperately to my inner tube, and pushing my face out of the water to gasp mouthfuls of air as the raging river rushed over me. I had just managed to lift myself back into my tube when a giant wave hit me square in the face and knocked me back into the water again. Holding on desperately with my right hand, I saw a giant rock looming straight ahead of me. I kicked my legs furiously and paddled weakly with my left hand in an attempt to avoid a collision. The current carried me inches past the rock and dumped me headfirst into a whirlpool known as the "Coffeepot."

I was too exhausted to pull myself back on the tube, but without the leverage the tube afforded, I could not escape from the whirlpool. It battered me back and forth several times, threatened to pull me underwater, and threw wave after wave into my face. Finally, for no reason at all that I could discern, it spat me free into the calm waters of an eddy. I gratefully paddled my way to the shallow water and regained the safety of my tube. I was gasping for breath. I was scared. I felt lucky to be alive and paralyzed with fear at the same time.

Moments later, my friend Catherine came riding by on her tube, expertly skirting the edge of the Coffeepot. Her face was beaming with excitement, and her whole being radiated intense pleasure. She threw her arms wide open in the joy of being alive, and called out to me, "Wasn't that the greatest ride in the world? Have you ever done anything so fabulous in your whole life? Don't you just love this? We are so lucky to be here!" And with that, the speeding current pushed her around the bend, and she disappeared from my sight.

At that moment, something miraculous changed for me. It was impossible for me to stay worried and scared in the presence of so much aliveness and celebration. Somehow,

Catherine's infectious sense of joy flooded me with a sense of my own happiness. I felt my whole being relax. The danger was over, and I was safe. The river looked beautiful, the forest was gorgeous, and my friends were calling me to join them in the fun.

I was grateful to Catherine for pulling me out of my troubled state, but I don't always get that from my friends, nor they from me. Usually when I'm feeling glorious about my life and I meet a friend who is having a difficult time, I try to tamp down my enthusiasm. I'm afraid that if he hears how well I'm doing, he'll only feel worse about himself. So I pretend that things are not going quite as well as they are. I talk about the places in my life where things are going badly for me, too, under the misguided theory that "misery loves company." If I leave feeling worse than when I arrived, we both feel like I've been a good friend.

Fortunately for us, dogs don't act that way. Dogs are always happy to share their passion about being alive. It's easy for them to lift our foul moods because dogs bring their joy with them wherever they go.

A dog entering a room is like Catherine floating by in her inner tube. Whenever Celeste prances into the living room and discovers someone already there, she gets tremendously excited. Her whole being lights up as soon as she spots me across the room, and she runs over to the couch, tail wagging joyfully, snuggling up as close as she can. She licks my face, and then she licks my hands when I hold them up to protect my face from her exuberant dog bath.

Her message is simple and irresistible: "I'm here now, so get out of your funk! It's time to get up and have some fun!"

*"Everything that is done in the world
is done by hope."*
—MARTIN LUTHER KING, JR.

DOGS KEEP

HOPING

My dogs find cheese irresistible. Whenever I take out a snack of cheese and crackers for myself, the dogs instantly sit right at my feet. They stare at me, watching every move with the rapt attention of a youngster playing a video game.

Some might say that my dogs are begging, but I prefer to believe that they are hoping. Not that begging and hoping are mutually exclusive, mind you. Personally, I think begging almost always involves at least some effort to induce guilt. Now, I don't mean to imply that I have anything against begging or guilt. I believe that some guilt can be very positive and helpful. The kind of guilt involved in begging can even be wholesome and a good learning experience as well. The Greek philosopher Diogenes was once asked, "Why, Diogenes, do you beg?"

"In order to teach people generosity," he quickly replied.

My wife would argue that my dogs are neither begging nor hoping for my cheese. According to her, they are simply waiting. She claims that the sharing of my cheese with the dogs is a foregone conclusion, and they know it. In order for there to be authentic hope, she says, then there must be always at least some chance that the object of hope will not be realized. Frankly, I think my wife is right about hope but wrong about the dogs. Even though they have always shared in my snacks in the past, I still think they aren't totally sure. My judgment is based upon the look in their eyes.

They get the very same look every time we take out the suitcases. As soon as we start to pack, the dogs begin to get very nervous. They look at us with enormous hope in their darting eyes. They are hoping for those three little words, "You can go!" My wife and I travel quite a bit, and I would guess that when we travel there is about a fifty-fifty chance that the dogs will be going along. As we prepare to leave, they follow our every move looking for some slight hint about their fate.

On those occasions that they are left behind, their hope is alive until the very last piece of luggage is loaded and I tell them, "You can't go. You stay here. We'll be back!" These are the same phrases I use every time I leave without them— whether I'm off to work or off to Europe. They clearly know what I mean. Invariably, I see the hope vanish instantly, and they collapse on the floor in disappointment and despair.

Several years ago when we sold our house, the dogs were particularly anxious. They knew that this was not an ordinary trip. Not only had the suitcases been brought out, but also the moving van had come and taken all the furniture and boxes. The dogs would not let us out of their sight. They were concerned; however they never lost hope. I saw their hope transformed into complete and unadulterated joy when I uttered the magic words—"You can go!"

I wish that we could recapture in our own lives the kind of hope that our dogs have. In the eighteenth century Alexander Pope wrote the famous line, "Hope springs eternal in the human breast." I wonder, however, if Pope would hold that same sentiment today. Modern times seem characterized more by cynicism and hopelessness than by hope.

To be hopeful is to be always ready for something that has not yet happened. Hope is the ability to look at the compost pile and see the possibility of flowers growing there someday. Real hope can even stare death in the face and say, "Life is still worth living."

Hope is my dog, waiting for those magic words that may never come, "You can go!"

*"The dog was created especially for children.
He is the god of frolic."*

—Henry Ward Beecher

Dogs Celebrate,
Celebrate,
Celebrate

One of the reasons that we find dogs so delightful is that they are constantly celebrating our arrival on the scene. When I go out to a restaurant for dinner, Blue and Celeste act like I've been gone for years when I return. They bark joyously and dash around the yard when they hear the car approaching the house. When my wife and I get out of the car they wag their tails furiously, wiggle and waggle their bodies in a wild little dance, and—in general—act like the most exciting thing in the world that could possibly happen has just happened.

The same thing is true when my friends come over for a visit. I like to make a big fuss over my friends, but it's nothing like the outrageous fuss that the dogs make over them. Every time the doorbell rings, the dogs act like the Prodigal Son has finally returned. Whenever someone comes to the door the dogs say, "Hey! Time for a giant celebration."

For that matter, I don't even have to leave in the car. When I return through the front door from picking up the morning newspaper, the dogs respond like I have just returned from Europe. Fifteen minutes later I might leave to empty the garbage, and the dogs go through their routine all over again. "He's back!" their whole beings seem to shout. For dogs, virtually every event is an invitation to celebrate.

Celebrating our milestones with friends is an important way to share our lives together. Birthdays, anniversaries, and holidays are wonderful times to focus on the people that are most important in our lives. These special events create memories that continue to nourish us for a long time, because they create a sacred space for laughter, tears, and the kind of reckless joy that comes from moving together through time as a community.

However, our dogs show us that something even more is possible for our lives. Dogs demonstrate that we don't have to wait for a special day, the annual company retreat, or the occasional retirement party in order to celebrate. Dogs are ready every moment of their lives—in an instant—to throw a celebration. For a dog, no event in life is too small to celebrate. My dogs, for example, eat the same meal at approximately the same time every night. The way my dogs celebrate this impending meal would make one think that it was the greatest feast day of the year!

Our lives would be filled with so much more joy and happiness if we could learn to see each new day, each contact with our friends, each moment with our families, or—for that matter—our time alone, as an opportunity to celebrate. We are all blessed with this remarkable experience that is known as "life," and that alone is something to celebrate, celebrate, celebrate!

*"Even if it is a little thing, do something
for those who have need of help."*

—ALBERT SCHWEITZER

DOGS ASK FOR

HELP

Whenever her ball rolls under the table, Celeste crouches down and attempts to squeeze her muzzle underneath the legs of the nearest chair. When she can't quite reach the ball, she stands up and stares at it intently for a few moments, making sure it's still there. Then she crouches down once more and tries again. But it's still no use. This time when she stands up, she backs away from the chair and looks over in my direction.

"Go ahead and try it again," I encourage her. "You can do it!"

Dubiously, she crouches down again, but the ball is still just beyond her reach. It's obviously hopeless to keep trying, so she prances over to where I am sitting, sits down in front of me, and looks at me imploringly. "C'mon," she seems to say to me, "I know you can help me out with this kind of thing. I've seen you do it before."

Wearily, I get up from my chair, walk over to the table, and lift the offending chair out of the way. Celeste gleefully pounces on the ball and struts around with it in her mouth. Problem solved! We're a team! Let the games continue!

Dogs don't have any difficulty asking for help. They don't need to maintain appearances. They don't need to look competent or protect their image of who they are. Dogs don't feel ashamed if they can't handle something all by themselves. If they need assistance in getting what they want, they just ask for it.

Asking for help can be difficult for us, because it makes us feel vulnerable. We don't know how other people will accept our pleas for assistance. Yet if we don't ask for the help that we really need, we miss opportunities for connection to other people. In all aspects of our lives—home, school, family relationships, work—there will be times when we need help from others.

I got a voice mail recently from Miles Valentino, Playfair's Director of Training, a few days before he was scheduled to begin his performing tour of college campuses around the country. Miles sent his message out to everyone on our voice-mail network, saying that he was stressed out and having some pretravel jitters. He asked if anyone else was experiencing the same problem, and, if so, what they were doing to calm their anxiety.

I sent Miles a response, giving him what advice I could, but mainly telling him how much I respected him for being so vulnerable in asking for help. A few days later, Miles called back to let me know that he had received lots of helpful responses and was feeling much better about preparing for his trip.

But the best part, he said, was all the messages of loving support he received that had nothing to do with solving his travel problems. Many of the facilitators who had once been his students had called to let him know how much they appreciated him. They told him that they carried his teachings in their hearts wherever they went and that a little piece of him was always there inside of them, making a difference even if he chose to stay at home and never travel again. They told him that they loved him and cared about him. They took the excuse of his reaching out to ask for help to tell him all sorts of appreciative things that they had never told him before, things that made him feel wonderful about himself.

Oftentimes, it's difficult to ask for help. But as Miles discovered, many times you get back a lot more than you asked for.

"The average dog is a nicer person than the average person."

—ANDREW A. ROONEY

DOGS DON'T BITE WHEN A GROWL WILL DO

When Blue was just a tiny puppy she had a nasty little growl. My wife and I figured that Blue, being the only female in a litter of eight, had learned fairly quickly to let the other puppies know just where she was coming from. When we brought her home she continued her habit of growling whenever things didn't go her way. Everyone started warning me that I should break her of the habit immediately. I thought it was cute, so I encouraged it.

By the time she was a few months old, Blue and I had turned her growling habit into a game. We especially delighted in playing our game for concerned onlookers. We would wrestle on the floor or on the bed, and Blue would bare her teeth and growl in a way that brought *The Exorcist* to mind. Just when it appeared that everything was totally out of control, I would lean close to Blue's face and say, "Don't you growl at me!" Without fail, she responded with a juicy lick on the end of my nose.

As Blue has grown to maturity, she has never given up her love of the growl. Her growl has ranged from very playful to very serious. I observed her serious growl on a number of occasions, most notably while she was rearing her own litter of puppies. However, never in her ten years of life has Blue's growl worsened to a bite. Dogs don't bite when a growl will do. Dogs don't take negative situations and escalate them into total disasters.

If only the average person were as nice as the average dog, things would go better for all of us. Unlike our dogs, we have a tendency to aggravate situations in ways that make them so much worse than they otherwise would be if we could stay calm. Many of us are living on the stressful edge, where even in ordinary situations we might be inclined to bite. Minor disagreements with sales clerks, coworkers, telephone solicitors, other drivers, and even our loved ones can quickly get out of hand. Our grumbling and growling can swiftly erupt into snarling rages where we feel like biting the other person's head off.

I saw a bumper sticker on a car in front of me recently that read, "Where are we all going? And why am I in a handbasket?" I got a good laugh from the bumper sticker, and I realized that it often seems to me that we are indeed "going to hell in a handbasket." So much of this feeling is due to our inability to maintain a state of peace and calm in our lives. An unknown author once wrote, "Peace does not mean to be in a place where there is no noise, trouble, or hard work. It means to be in the midst of those things and still be calm in your heart." One of the most liberating feelings we can experience is to know that we humans have that choice.

When someone is yelling in my face and invading my personal space, the easiest thing is to yell right back. But I try to remember that my job is to help ease a difficult situation, rather than to escalate it. When outside observers report that a fight was averted because "cooler heads prevailed," I want it to be my head they're talking about.

We all have the capacity to choose a life of peace and calm even while the world around us is going to hell in a handbasket. On occasion, grumbling and growling a bit when things don't go our way can serve a useful purpose in voicing our displeasure. On the other hand, like our dogs, we don't ever have to bite when a simple growl will do.

"Criticism is prejudice made plausible."
—H. L. MENCKEN

DOGS TAKE
CRITICISM WITHOUT
RESENTMENT

Having a young golden retriever means that almost certainly you will return home a few times to find your shoes, your books, or perhaps your whole fence eaten. They love to chew on things. Several people have told me that golden retrievers "mature slowly." That is clearly an understatement. In my experience, if your golden retriever stops chewing things by the time she is four, you are ahead of most golden guardians.

My wife and I have come to accept that a few chewed belongings just go with the territory. When we return to our home and find one of our prized books chomped on and spread all over the house, we take it surprisingly well. We have learned to laugh on the inside and say, "such is life." However, we put on a great theatrical display for the dogs.

"Oh my! Look at this! Who did this?" one of us will shout. "Come look at this!" we say to the dogs. "Who did this?" We are close to certain that Celeste had no part in it. It's just not a poodle thing. We are reasonably sure that Blue is innocent. She outgrew that stage a few years back. We are virtually positive that Mead, our young golden pup, is the culprit.

However, all three dogs, who at first run to greet us, hunker down in wretched, pitiful shame. If one had to pick the guilty party on the basis of the hangdog looks, it would be a toss-up. All three have tails tucked, heads bowed, and eyes darting this way and that. Blue and Celeste look so guilty that I am almost converted from my previous conviction about Mead.

Our drama continues as we clean up the mess. "I can't believe what I am seeing! A dog ate my book! How could this be?" I suppose that this is more than a bit unfair to the innocent; however, dogs are so good-natured about receiving criticism that I know that one simple word will transform the whole situation for both guilty and innocent, alike. When they hear, "O.K.," they instantly come running with tails wagging and smiles on their faces. Innocent or guilty, they are—without hesitation—our real friends again.

You won't find our dogs moping around or harboring ill feelings just because they have been criticized. Their motto is surely, "Hey, if you're O.K., then I'm O.K."

For most human beings, being criticized is a problem of cosmic significance. Most of us just don't like being criticized by anyone about anything. That's why we often end up resenting those who criticize us.

For most of us, our parents were the first people to criticize us, and—especially if we had highly critical parents—this means we are likely to unconsciously associate any criticism with parental disapproval. That's why we often get upset when people in positions of authority are critical of us. Singer, song-writer, and psychologist Peter Alsop asks his audiences, "Do you know why it is so easy for our parents to push our buttons?" His answer is, "Because they are the ones who installed them!"

In some cases people who criticize us are doing so because they are deeply concerned about our well-being. In those cases, they might be doing us a favor because we might have something to learn from their critical feedback.

Much of the time, however, our critics are merely reacting from their own insecurity. If people who do not really care about us are criticizing us because they themselves are insecure, jealous, or just plain nasty, we can recognize that they are speaking to us out of their own unhappiness. Why should we make ourselves unhappy in response to their unhappiness?

Epictetus, the Stoic philosopher, urged his disciples not to be afraid of the criticism of others. He argued that we cannot control the impressions that other people form of us, and the effort to defend ourselves only debases our character. Epictetus's wry recommendation was that if you hear that somebody has criticized you, do not bother with excuses or defenses, just smile and say, "I guess that person does not know all my other faults. Otherwise, he would not have mentioned only these."

Clearly, one of the most effective ways to respond to criticism is to respond exactly as our dogs do. We can just hunker down and listen. If the criticism doesn't teach us anything useful about ourselves, we don't have to resent it—we can just let go of it. In fact, maybe the best thing you can do the next time someone's criticism makes you feel upset or resentful is to ask yourself, "Now, how would my dog handle this?" Just asking the question will probably make you laugh out loud.

"The greatest pleasure of a dog is that you may make a fool of yourself with him, and not only will he not scold you, but he will make a fool of himself too."

—SAMUEL BUTLER

DOGS DON'T MIND BEING THE BUTT OF A JOKE

My wife and I had huge grins on our faces when we dressed Blue up in a party hat and sunglasses for her birthday photograph. Blue barked delightedly as soon as the flash went off and then dashed around the yard in her hat and glasses, to everyone's entertainment.

We get an even bigger laugh every night when, after my wife flosses her own teeth, she flosses Celeste's teeth as well. The way Celeste sits down and stares attentively, waiting her turn as soon as the floss makes its appearance, always makes us smile. The way she excitedly bites at the tiny strand of floss as it moves through her big teeth makes us laugh out loud. The way she wags her tail, obviously having a good time throughout the whole thing, is a can't-fail source of entertainment for us every evening.

Is this a case of "we're laughing at you, not with you"? Well, sort of. But the dogs don't mind at all. What's important to them is that there is fun happening, and that they are having as much fun as we are. They are happy to sacrifice their dignity so that everyone can have a good time. If dogs were comedians, then taking a pie in the face would be their best routine. "Anything for fun" is their motto. Like Shakespeare's Falstaff, dogs can take pride in being "not only witty in myself, but the cause that wit is in other men."

A few months ago, I was being introduced to an audience of more than two thousand people at a conference in Tampa. The woman introducing me was very generously building me up as someone really important with many credentials. Just as she was finishing, I looked down and noticed that my pants were unzipped. I tried very quickly and unobtrusively to zip up my pants before walking on stage. That was when I discovered that the zipper was broken.

There were two huge twenty-foot screens on both sides of the room, which would be projecting my closed-circuit image for all to see. I am very animated when I speak, always walking the entire stage and often into the audience. I could not imagine standing behind the podium to hide my zipper problem. So, I walked onto the stage, and the first thing I did was tell the audience that one would think that a person with all those impressive credentials could at least keep his pants zipped. I explained my broken zipper story as the audience roared with laughter at my expense.

The interesting thing that I noticed that day was that the audience was with me from the very beginning. We were totally connected. Throughout my presentation, the cameraman occasionally panned down to get a good shot of my zipper and the audience let out another roar. We had a great time together that day. My zipper dilemma turned out to be a wonderful way to bond with the audience and instantly have their full support. I'm sure that my willingness to be the butt of the joke was central to the success of my presentation that day.

There are many ways that we can use laughter and play to break through the artificial barriers that separate us as human beings. When we show other people that we don't take ourselves too seriously, it is contagious. If we can feel comfortable with being the butt of a joke, we can help other people to lighten up as well. And we get to see once again that acting like a dog can actually make us feel more human with each other.

"If you can start the day without caffeine...
If you can get going without pep pills...
If you can eat the same food every day
and be grateful for it... If you can conquer
the world tension without medical help...
If you can relax without liquor... If you
can sleep without the aid of drugs...
Then my friend, you are almost
as good as your dog."

—AUTHOR UNKNOWN

DOGS ARE

HEALTHY

According to *Pocket English Idioms*, when one is as "sick as a dog" one is "very sick with a cold, flu, or stomach problem." In my own recollections, whenever someone has used the phrase "sick as a dog," then they weren't just feeling a bit poorly, they were bedridden, commode-hugging unwell. I don't know about you, but in my experience dogs are remarkably healthy creatures. I don't have any hard-core statistics to offer regarding pets' physical health, but if early mortality rates are any indication, then "sick as a fish" makes a lot more sense.

I will grant that you can't start analyzing idioms too carefully because few of them make much sense. We hear that it is a "dog eat dog" world. I have had a dog who would eat broccoli and bananas, and who would die for Brie, but I have never had or known of a dog that would even consider eating another dog. I think that Juvenal had it right when he wrote, "dog does not eat dog."

Then, of course, we hear of someone or another being "in the doghouse," which we understand to mean that the person is in big trouble. However, in reality the doghouse is a quite comfortable place if one happens to be a dog. The doghouse is a place to protect dogs and provide them shelter against the elements. If you are not a dog and hang out in doghouses anyway, then you richly deserve to be in whatever kind of trouble you have found yourself!

The other most popular idiom involving dogs advises that we should take care to "let sleeping dogs lie." Personally, if I followed this advice, then my dogs and I would not have much of a relationship at all. I've never calculated the hours in a day that my dogs sleep; however, I think it is fairly safe to say that if I didn't rouse them from their sleep for one activity or another, then they would likely sleep better than twenty-three hours a day. In fact, if you have a dog, then I wager there is a pretty good chance that he or she is asleep at this very moment.

It is not, of course, that idioms involving dogs are the only ones that do not hold up well under close scrutiny. All my life I have heard of people who are "happy as a clam," "drunk as a skunk," or "blind as a bat." I don't think an in-depth examination is necessary to understand that these are wacko ideas, as well.

My dogs do throw up now and again. This invariably happens when they undertake what I consider to be the fairly bizarre behavior of eating grass. An old folktale suggests that dogs eat grass as a barf-inducing technique when they are experiencing an upset stomach. This could explain the "sick as a dog" idiom, I suppose.

There is, however, absolutely no evidence to support the idea that this is why dogs eat grass. Scientists who have given their rapt attention to this pressing question have concluded that dogs eat grass for one of two reasons. They say it could be that the dogs' wolf heritage is involved. In this view, wolves fed on animals that were herbivores and, therefore, frequently ate the grasses that were in the stomachs of their prey. Hence, it was natural for wolves and their descendants to learn to like grass.

The second, and much simpler, explanation is that dogs just like the taste of grass, so they eat it, and this causes them to upchuck. My own hypothesis is simpler yet. My dogs know by my fits of hysteria that I don't like for them to eat grass. So, they do it just to pull my chain. It's part of the old forbidden-fruit syndrome that they have rightfully picked up from us by being our closest companions.

In any case, on those occasions when my dogs do eat grass and then come inside for their obligatory vomit on the carpet, that's the end of it. They are, shall we say, happy as clams watching me clean up the mess. No sign of sickness follows the purge.

In case you are wondering about my point in all this discourse, here it is: Dogs are quite healthy and, in fact, provide us with a rather wonderful model of both physical and emotional health. Dogs have good health practices. Clearly they get plenty of rest, and if they aren't eating a sensible diet and getting plenty of exercise, then whom exactly should we hold responsible? I suggest that a glance in the mirror holds the not-so-mysterious answer.

Our dogs are not just themselves hale and hearty, but also they are good for our health. Research now shows that the simple act of petting a dog is good for both our mental and physical well-being. Petting a dog eases our tension and lowers stress. It also lowers our heart rate and releases endorphins. So, if you want to feel better and be healthier, then go pet a dog. Of course, you should feel free to ignore this sage advice. But don't say that you haven't been forewarned. You may end up sick as a fish!

"If we were as apathetic as many humans, then someone would probably suggest putting us to sleep."

—*Conversations with Dog*

Dogs Are Enthusiastic and Energetic

Casey Bear and Sweet Dreams had been my running companions for many years when Blue arrived on the scene. From Blue's first day out, she showed an enthusiasm for running that was unmatched by any dog I had ever seen. This dog loved to run! Even though the other dogs were much older, Blue simply had to be the leader of the pack as we ran down the Ridgeline Trail.

Blue loves running so much that whenever I go to the closet to select my shoes, she gets very interested. If I pull out any pair of shoes other than my running shoes, Blue gives me a ho-hum look and doesn't move from the comfortable spot in her favorite chair. However when I pull out the running shoes, she becomes a different dog.

At the first sight of a running shoe, Blue bounds out of the chair and starts running around in circles. She starts leaping in the air with all four feet off of the ground. She rushes to the other room, grabs her own leash, and comes running back with a huge smile on her face.

Of course, Blue—and other golden retrievers—may be among the most enthusiastic and energetic of all dogs. However, most dogs have much to teach us when it comes to showing passion for life. In my experience, every great teacher that I have ever known has had enormous passion for what they do. I think a large part of being happy is finding something in our lives that inspires and energizes us the way that running motivates Blue.

So many people whom I meet these days seem to operate with a practiced nonchalance about everything in life. *Whatever*, is their favorite word. I don't believe this kind of indifference and unresponsiveness is going to lead them to much happiness. We may mistakenly think that not caring about anything is a way to protect ourselves from the pain that comes with being vulnerable to life, but I'm not sure it can lead to much more than a life of continual misery. A life without passion and enthusiasm is drained of much of what makes life worth living.

As Aristotle and so many other great thinkers have pointed out for us, habit strongly shapes our lives. The behaviors that we practice over and over again begin to have an energy all their own. If we are habitually cold and unconcerned about most things in life, then we will soon take that same attitude toward things that really *do* matter. Unless we are willing to say with unbounded conviction about at least a few things, "This counts for something!" then soon our whole life will count for nothing.

When I return home from a walk with the dogs, as soon as I open the front gate they dash through and run as fast as they can to the front door. Obviously they can't get through the front door until I open it, so there's no advantage to getting there before I do. But that makes no difference to them. Their madcap enthusiasm at the end of our walk is totally infectious. No matter how tired I may be, I am always reenergized by their antics.

Then, as soon as I open the door, they run to greet my wife and tell her that we're home. They let her know that she really, really matters to them. When she sees the passionate wiggling and waggling of the dogs' bodies and their excitement about making contact, their enthusiasm invariably lifts her spirits.

We can do the same thing for the people we care about. In our own way, we can run to greet them and shower them with love anytime we see them. I've been trying out this approach more and more often with the people in my life, and most of them seem to appreciate it. When I walk through the door right after the dogs, I try to match the dogs' enthusiasm with a passionate greeting of my own, and my wife really responds to it.

Except when I get carried away and lick her in the face. There are some areas where it's just no use trying to compete with the dogs.

"Home is where the heart is."

—ANGELA CARTER

DOGS ALWAYS
COME HOME

During my college years I was of the opinion that it was cruel and unusual punishment to lock my dog indoors while I went to class. So the last thing I would do as I headed off to school in the morning was to lead my dog, Madeline, into the front yard and tell her to stay. She stood quite forlornly watching me walk off into the distance as I waved a last good-bye. However, as I soon discovered, she didn't stay in the yard for long.

We lived about ten blocks from campus, and my college friends took great delight in spotting Madeline secretly roaming the school grounds at all hours of the day. She made sure to find her way back to our house, though, before I did. When I returned home for dinner she was innocently waiting on the front steps, eagerly wagging her tail in greeting as though she'd been there the whole day.

After graduation I moved to the big city, and Madeline quite easily adapted to the life of an urban dog. Madeline was quite fearless in her exploration of the neighborhood where we lived. Early one evening my housemate got a call from a Good Samaritan who found her wandering alone about forty blocks from our house. When I arrived home from work a few hours later, I was horrified to find that my housemate hadn't bothered to go get Madeline. Instead, he had assured the caller that Madeline could find her own way home just fine. "Just let her go," my roommate advised the caller.

After a few more hours had passed without any sign of the dog, I was even more furious with my irresponsible housemate and told him so in no uncertain terms. But letting out my anger didn't calm me down much—I was still quite beside myself with worry. Eventually I had to give up my vigil and go to sleep, but I left the front door slightly ajar in the hope that Madeline would somehow find her way home, nose open the door, and let herself in. Sure enough, at about three in the morning, I was awakened to the sound of a pack of dogs on the run. Dogs of all shapes and sizes came crashing up the stairs into my third-floor bedroom with Madeline in the lead. She not only had opened the front door and let herself in, she had invited all her friends over for a party!

I was not in a partying mood, so I chased the traveling menagerie back out the front door. I hated to admit that my idiot roommate had been right, but after that I never again doubted Madeline's abilities to find her way home.

Several years later when I paid a visit to my old college town, I took Madeline with me. I left her at the house of some friends while I attended my meetings on campus. When I returned to pick her up, I discovered once again that Madeline was lost. No one had seen her for several hours, and when I questioned them, my friends engaged in some heated finger-pointing.

"I thought you said you would watch the dog!"

"No, you told me you were going to watch the dog!"

I wandered fruitlessly around the neighborhood for several hours calling out Madeline's name, but it was hopeless. Then I had a sudden inspiration. The house where I had lived in college was several miles away on the opposite end of town. I got in my car and drove through the familiar streets. There, waiting for me on the front porch like the intervening years had never happened, was Madeline. Once again, she had found her way home.

Finding one's way back home is perhaps the single greatest metaphor in all of history for the challenge of the human journey. Our task as human beings today is still that of Homer's Odysseus—finding our way home to our true self. Once we find our way home, we are able to fully love ourselves and other beings. Finding our way home means that we are able to live our lives with meaning, hope, comfort, and happiness. Finding our way home opens our heart to all that life has to offer.

Living with our dogs and being loved by our dogs opens

our hearts as well. In this way our dogs can help us to find our true home. They shower us with their affection and we, in turn, respond with our own. Each day with our dogs gives us endless opportunities to love and feel loved.

"In dog years, I'm dead."

—AUTHOR UNKNOWN

DOGS, EVEN OLD ONES, CAN LEARN NEW TRICKS

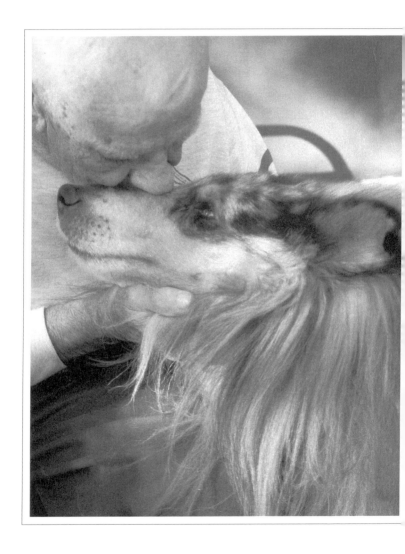

On two separate occasions my wife and I have lived for extended periods in Mexico. The first time we lived in a very small village of only about nine thousand people. At that time we had both Blue and Sweet Dreams, and they, of course, moved to Mexico with us.

On the very first night that we walked down the main street to the town square, many curious children quickly surrounded us. I'm fairly sure that they had never seen dogs on leashes, and they told us that they had only seen a dog like Blue—a purebred golden retriever—on television and in the movies. They were very impressed.

Then they turned their attention to Sweet Dreams. *"Es una borrega?"* The fact that they thought our big old standard poodle was a lamb would have really pleased me when we first got her some twelve years before, back in the days when I was embarrassed about being seen with a poodle. Now, however, it just made me laugh.

We assured the children that we were not out walking with a lamb and that both Blue and Sweet Dreams were dogs. For the next several months when we took our evening walk to the square, the children clamored to have their turn to walk the dogs around the plaza. They treated Blue and Sweet Dreams like big celebrities.

Living in a new and different culture can be a very difficult and stressful undertaking. Blue adapted to life in Mexico the most quickly of the four of us. Within two or three days, she had picked up the very distinctive manner of barking of the Mexican dogs in the village, and she barked like a native. Blue accepted her new Spanish name, *Azulita*, and quickly responded to all my commands in both English and Spanish.

For Sweet Dreams the adjustment was not so swift. I guess this was understandable for, as they say, in "dog years" she was ninety-one at the time. She clearly didn't care for the loud firecrackers that exploded at unpredictable hours, both night and day. When we referred to her by her Spanish name, *Dulce*, she gave us a look that said, "Surely you jest!" Yet, this sweet old dog was willing to learn some new tricks.

My wife and I rented our Mexican house solely on the basis of a description by the owners and a few photographs. It was a wonderful house, but one surprise was that there was a thirty-foot spiral staircase from the second to the third floor with only a small landing halfway up. Our bedroom was on the third floor.

When we arrived, Blue bounded up the staircase with grace, confidence, and more ease than I did. Truth be known, it was a little scary to me at first. Sweet Dreams slowly and very hesitantly followed us up to check out the new bedroom. Slowly and carefully she wound her way to the top.

The return trip was not as smooth. Blue led the way down with no difficulty, as my wife and I gingerly took it one step at a time with a bit of white knuckle support from the thin railing. Sweet Dreams, however, just stood and stared. As I called encouragement up to her, I noticed that her legs were beginning to quiver. She knew that she needed to come down, but she was gripped with fear.

No amount of coaxing, cajoling, or commanding could get her to move down the stairs. I went downstairs and retrieved one of her favorite cookies and then went back up and stood just below her. I held out the cookie and encouraged her to try. No chance.

I decided that I had no option but to pick her up and carry her down, which was quite unsettling to me. I was barely negotiating this winding stairway with confidence myself, and I wasn't too keen on doing it with a nervous, sixty-pound dog in my arms. When I went to gather her shaking body into my arms, she was so afraid that she wet all over both of us. I didn't particularly look forward to having to repeat this routine for the next several months.

Naturally, the next time that we went up the stairs, Sweet

Dreams followed. When we came back down she once again stood at the top of the stairs, looked down, and shook with fear. This time, however, I decided to just sit down and wait. After a few minutes she gave a short little bark as if to say, "Ah, excuse me! I think you forgot something up here." However, I didn't budge. I just called out encouragement, "Come on, Sweetie, you can do it."

About twenty minutes passed, and then I heard her first uncertain, tentative step down. Then, I heard another. I stole a glance up at her and noticed that even as she took the next hesitant step, her back legs were still shaking. I was so proud of this courageous old poodle!

She slowly wound her way all the way down and then leapt to the floor boldly from the third step. Blue was the first to congratulate her, and then my wife and I hugged her and showered her with praise. She looked at us as if to say, "What's the big deal? It's just a little ole staircase!" Within a couple of days, Sweet Dreams was descending the staircase with the same grace and confidence as Blue.

As we get older, we have a tendency to get stuck in comfortable patterns and familiar ways of doing things. So often we are afraid to try new things, take risks, and make ourselves vulnerable because we are afraid of change. We let our fear stand in the way of new learning and great adventures, which have the potential to bring us much happiness in our lives. We even tell ourselves that we can't learn anymore.

The reality is that we can all continue to learn and grow until the day we die. While it is very important to get physical exercise, exercising the brain is actually an equally important factor for ensuring a long, happy life. According to neuropsychologist Margery Hulter Silver, continuing to acquire new skills and knowledge actually develops new cellular connections in our brains. So, as we learn new things we are actually creating a "brain reserve" that can buffer and delay the onset of many age-related diseases.

Simply put, if we want to be as happy as we can be for as

long as we can be, then we have to be open all the time to new experiences. We must continue throughout our lives to seek out new challenges. We have to stay involved in life. We have to learn new tricks.

Sometimes we even have to attempt things that fill us with fear and make us want to wet all over ourselves.

"Heaven goes by favor. If it went by merit, you would stay out and your dog would go in."

—MARK TWAIN

DOGS DON'T COMPARE THEMSELVES TO OTHERS

Celeste is having a bad hair day, and it's all my fault. I took Celeste to the groomer and told them I wanted a different look—something fresh, something new. "Why does she always have to look like a poodle?" I asked. "Let's try something else!"

It seemed like a great idea, but when I returned several hours later Celeste looked awful. As soon as I saw her, I knew I had made a terrible mistake. I tried to calm myself down. "Okay, in a couple of days it will all grow out," I rationalized. "She'll look just fine. It just takes time to get used to something new."

But the succeeding days made Celeste look even worse. Her face was square, and every time she took a drink the water dripped down from the little beard on her muzzle. She started to smell mildewed, and when she gave me a kiss I smelled mildewed, too.

It was five weeks until her next haircut appointment. She was not only going to have a bad hair day—she was going to have a bad hair month! Her brother Sam came over for a visit, and next to his sharp poodle face, Celeste looked like a complete dork. I shot her an anguished look that said, "Can you ever forgive me?"

But Celeste didn't seem to care at all. She glanced back at me with an exasperated look that said, "What are you staring at? Get over it! Open the door already! Let's go out and have some fun!"

Dogs don't make comparisons about what they look like, whereas we humans are often obsessed with comparing ourselves to everyone we meet. Nowhere is this truer than at the fitness club, where our bodies are exposed for all to see.

I recently spent some time at a health spa. My favorite fitness class was called "Latin Aerobics." Two buff, gorgeous instructors in their early thirties, a man and a woman, who were fabulous dancers, led the class. The whole class was shimmying and shaking along with the music, and it was pretty easy to imagine that we were all moving exactly like the teachers were moving.

The problem was that the classroom was a dance studio that was covered with mirrors. Whenever I actually sneaked a look at myself in the mirror, I realized that what I was doing did not look very much like what the teachers were doing at all. They were moving their arms, they were moving their legs, and so was I—but that's about where the resemblance ended. This was especially true when I caught a glimpse of my so-called shimmy. I started thinking to myself, "I wish I really could dance like the two of them. It would be so great to walk into a party and be able to move the way they can move!" Then I'd sneak another peek in the mirror, and I'd think, "Forget it!"

I had been invited to give a lecture to the entire faculty of the spa, so I had to leave the class a few minutes before it ended to get ready for my own presentation. I took a shower and walked over to the lecture hall, and much to my delight, there were my two Latin aerobics instructors seated in the audience. I gave them a big smile, and walked over to tell them how much I had enjoyed their class.

I noticed that my two instructors tensed up as soon as I started walking over to them. They blurted out in panicked voices, one on top of the other, "Please don't call on us during this class!"

"Don't make us say anything!"

"We're not smart—we're all brawn and no brains. . . ."

"Don't embarrass us in front of everybody!"

"Please don't make us say anything stupid!"

I was completely shocked by their reaction. A half an hour before I had looked at them as if they could do no wrong. They were the picture of confidence, and now they were acting like scared little kids. What had happened to those two all-powerful instructors whom I had hero-worshipped from afar? What was going on?

Now that we had moved to my territory, the roles had obviously reversed. When I compared myself to them during the dance class, I found myself coming up short—there was no way I could hope to be as good as they were, so my comparing mind made me feel bad about myself. But they didn't even have to see me in action to make the same judgments about themselves—as soon as they set foot in my classroom, they felt inadequate about their own intellectual abilities.

Dogs don't have the same problem. I can't imagine my dog thinking, "Gee, I wish I had a body like that German shepherd!" My dog will never be a German shepherd, and I will never have the body of a thirty-year-old again. Neither of these facts needs to cause either of us any pain. That is just the way things are.

You can always make yourself feel bad if you start comparing yourself to someone else. On a given day, there will always be someone smarter than you, or richer than you, or more graceful than you. But so what? Once you learn to shut off your comparing mind, you can begin to relax and look around for the things that make you happy to be where you are, instead of the things that make you miserable.

"I wonder what goes through his mind when he sees us peeing in his water bowl."

—PENNY WARD MOSER

DOGS DON'T NEED DESIGNER WATER— AN OPEN TOILET SEAT WILL DO

I remember as a young man how utterly cool I thought it was when I watched the giant movie screen as James Bond ordered his martini "shaken but not stirred." These days, Agent 007's demands would be rather ordinary. I've heard people order a drink or a meal that sounded much more like they were providing specifications for the building of a new house.

My dogs, on the other hand, are not the least bit persnickety about food or drink. Oh, you can be sure that they are quite excited when they get an extra special treat. However, they are not the least bit demanding. They gratefully accept whatever comes their way.

When it comes to food, our golden retriever Casey Bear remains the prime example of my most nondiscriminating and grateful friend. In our family we had a saying, "If it is airborne food, then Casey will love it."

I think it started one evening when we were eating popcorn. Casey was sitting patiently but eyeing each handful as we all gobbled it down. Her head followed each move as though she were watching the most interesting tennis match in the history of sport. Finally, my son lobbed a kernel in her direction. Casey, who had never demonstrated unusual skill in catching balls or Frisbees, easily snagged the kernel and wagged her tail like we had just given her some filet mignon.

From that day forward, it became a great family game. It didn't matter if it was squash or sushi. If we fired a food projectile, then Casey unfailingly grabbed the morsel before it hit the floor. My son developed the behind-the-back broccoli, the between-the-legs banana, and the eyes-closed, backward, over-the-shoulder bagel shots. Casey never missed and never failed to show her deep gratitude for whatever came her way.

I'm not saying that our lives will be better if we become as indiscriminate as Casey Bear. Nor am I suggesting that there is anything wrong with having things the way that we like them. However, I think that at times we use our desire to have things "just so" merely as a way to feel special. This can often lead to chronic unhappiness.

The ancient philosopher Aristippus was a pleasure seeker of great repute. His immoderate exploits make today's "sex, drugs, and rock and roll" crowd look like amateur fun seekers. On the other hand, Aristippus taught that we must learn how to be just as satisfied and happy when what we take to be the greatest pleasures are not available to us. If we accustom ourselves to having things just the way we want them, then we're likely to feel unhappy when we can't have things our own way. Surely, those days will come along.

Being special is not about acquiring extraordinary things or making unique demands. It is really about a certain kind of deep awareness of oneself. When we understand that we are already special without having to change anything at all about who we are, then we can loosen up, lighten up, and let go. We no longer need to prove it to ourselves or anyone else. As Alan Watts used to say, there is great wisdom in recognizing that "you are already It."

"I am a dog. You are a man. You expect too much.
I accept too little. Even when I get too little,
I still know that life is good.
Too often you overlook that fact."

—CONVERSATIONS WITH DOG

DOGS DON'T GET
STUCK IN THE
NEGATIVE

The upbeat character of a dog is one of her most endearing attributes. Dogs are rarely depressed. In fact, even when things go wrong, dogs stay very positive. When they are confronted with the negative, they don't get stuck there. If dogs could speak English, then I am certain that they would have been the ones to invent the phrase, "Get over it!"

Often people will ask me if my dogs are "house dogs." I'm never quite sure how to respond. I feel it is almost as if I have been asked, "Are your children house children?"

Yes, my dogs are house dogs. They get down off the couch only to get into the bed. Sometimes they even get under the covers.

It's not that my dogs don't go outside. In fact, often they go to the back door and scratch the door. Usually this is an indication that they are hot and would like to go out and take a refreshing dip in the swimming pool.

On the other hand, my dogs also love the woods. My wife and I live in a heavily wooded area, and we have also spent many nights over the years vacationing, backpacking, and sleeping in the woods. My dogs love to run through the forest investigating every hole and every smell. At these times, I actually think that they fashion themselves as authentic hunters—wild animals who must track down their prey. I allow them this illusion and don't tease or shame them when they come running back to the house for their evening gourmet meal.

Squirrels, of course, are their usual quarries; however, over the years they have tracked everything from antelope to wild boar. Blue did catch a squirrel once or twice. Most often, however, their adventures in the woods lead to nothing more than a fun chase and low-hanging tongues.

That was before Sweet Dreams flushed out a skunk. My wife and I were vacationing in a luxurious Colorado mountain cabin. We were taking an evening walk in the cool, refreshing air. The dogs were absorbed in the hunt. They were about fifty yards away from us when we spotted the skunk.

I remember it still as though it were all happening in slow motion. The skunk was moving away as fast as possible, which wasn't very fast. Sweetie and Blue were following the skunk and trying to smell the skunk's rear as if it were the Pomeranian next door. I screamed frantically, "No! Sweetie, Blue, no! Come!"

For one of the few times in her life, Blue actually listened to me and came running back. Sweet Dreams, on the other hand, could not be bothered. My giant poodle was tracking her prey.

Then I saw it. A giant cloud of skunk mist enveloped Sweetie's head. The skunk had tired of the chase and let Sweet Dreams have it right in the face. It didn't take Sweetie long to decide that the fun was over. Enough was enough. She ran back toward the house, thinking, no doubt, that it was time to climb back on the couch in our lavish digs and sort things out.

I had other ideas, however. Sweet Dreams smelled so strongly of skunk that there was no way I could let her back into the house without a bath. I could barely stand to get close enough to her to wet her down.

Sweetie never cared much for baths unless they were pro-vided in the plush surroundings of the indoor grooming salon. She had not yet accepted the concept of the outdoor bath. This time, however, I gave her no choice.

The first bath had no discernible effect upon the smell. Instead of smelling like a skunk, Sweetie now just smelled like a wet skunk. Baths two and three had the same result. I realized that our regular dog shampoo was not designed for fighting this kind of an overpowering odor. So I drove into town and returned with a large bottle of strawberry shampoo.

Baths numbers four and five left us with a poodle that smelled like a sweet, strawberry-scented skunk. At this point we made an emergency call to the vet. Sweet Dreams stood outside looking through the door totally perplexed. "What's the problem?" her look seemed to say. "Clear me some space on the couch! What's the deal?"

The vet was not all that encouraging. "Try using some tomato juice, baking soda, vinegar, and perhaps some lemon; however, it will probably just take some time for the smell to totally go away."

We didn't have time. It was getting dark fast. The only times that Sweet Dreams had slept outside was when we were sleeping outside with her in a tent. Neither my wife nor I had any intention of spending the night out on the porch with Sweetie. My wife insisted that we couldn't bring her inside until the smell was history. After all, we were renting someone else's house.

Baths six, seven, and eight involved strange concoctions of all the things the vet had suggested. Nothing worked. Through it all, however, Sweet Dreams stayed positive about the whole situation. She couldn't understand why she had suddenly been banished from the house and punished with repeated baths in the cold air, but she made the best of it.

My wife and I spent a restless and nearly sleepless night. Time and again I got up to check on Sweetie. She was dozing away comfortably on the porch, apparently unfazed. Her ninth bath the next morning combined with a brisk walk through the woods finally allowed Sweetie to successfully pass the sniff test. Once I opened the front door, she headed gratefully for the couch.

We humans have a tendency to wallow in the negative aspects of life. We spend a lot more time worrying about what's going wrong than celebrating what's going right. That's why the whole skunk affair seemed much more traumatic for us than for Sweet Dreams. She remained positive in the face of the negative, even when she received a full blast of negativity right in the face. Once again, my dogs reminded me about the importance of staying positive in the face of adversity—even when life stinks!

"Happiness is a warm puppy."

—CHARLES M. SCHULTZ

DOGS ARE EASILY ENTERTAINED

Every time that the dog count around our house stays at two for very long, I start nagging my wife about getting a puppy. She always objects that we can't possibly get another dog—especially a puppy. Just as I have learned over the years to count on her response, she has come to expect mine. "Just what are we going to do on a three-dog night when we are caught with only two dogs?" She is never even mildly amused. Eventually, however, she always gives in.

Such is the way that we came to have the newest member of our family, a seven-month old rescue dog. We named her Mead after another golden retriever that my wife had many years ago. The earlier Mead was a very special dog to my wife and died prematurely of cancer. Both Meads are namesakes of the famous anthropologist Margaret Mead.

Having Mead around the house reminds me daily of how easily dogs are entertained. Just the other day I watched with considerable amusement and delight as Mead entertained herself with a feather that she discovered in the yard.

Like most pups, her first inclination was to chew on it. She chewed for a long while before apparently deciding that this was not a chewing feather but rather a tossing feather. So she tossed it in the air numerous times thinking, perhaps, that a feather doesn't really need a bird attached in order to fly.

Much to my surprise, it turned out that she was right, for a gust of wind caught the feather and blew it into the air. Mead took off in wild pursuit and enjoyed a great game of chase until the wind subsided and delivered her toy back to her on the ground. She responded by holding the feather in place with her paw and giving it a nearly interminable licking.

Alas, even the most enjoyable of entertainments must eventually reach its conclusion, and so Mead left the well-licked feather in search of some other plaything. However, she was no more than a few steps away when another thought apparently crossed her mind. She scooped up the feather in her mouth, ran over into the garden, and promptly buried it. Whether or not this was the final interment or merely a fine place to store the feather for some future joy is known only to Mead.

The enormous amount of entertainment that Mead found with this simple feather made me think of how much happier we all would be if we could be so easily amused. For many years now, though, almost everyone I know has been headed in exactly the opposite direction—seeking more and more ways to be entertained but finding it to be a very difficult and complex undertaking.

When we were very young children, all of us had a Meadlike capacity to be entertained by simple things. Parents of young children all tell the same story. The parents buy their child a fancy new toy, and when they return to the child's room ten minutes later, the toy has been discarded, and the child is having a grand old time playing with the box in which the toy came!

But as we grow older, most people seem to forget that life itself can still be endlessly interesting. Whether listening to a Walkman, playing a video game, or watching the latest giant flat screen television, most of us spend our lives surrounded by expensive gadgets and gizmos to keep us perpetually entertained. Soon we feel lost without all this external stimulation.

Fortunately, we never really lose our ability to see the things around us as if for the first time, to view all of life with childlike wonder. We don't have to replace our CD collection with a feather collection, or make any other changes to the external circumstances of our lives. When we practice looking at the world again with this "beginner's mind," then everything we encounter can make us as happy as a puppy.

"I think dogs are the most amazing creatures.
For me they are the role model
for being alive."

—GILDA RADNER

DOGS ARE
HAPPY WITH A
SIMPLE LIFE

Santosa—meaning "contentment regardless of outer cir-cumstances"—is among the most important of universal spiritual principles. My dogs just happen to be *Santosa* masters. In fact, it appears to me that they need only three things to make them happy. They are social animals, so they need time to be in the company of others. They love to rest and relax, so they need a place to lie down, preferably a dry one. Finally, they require ample food and water—nothing fancy mind you, just enough to keep up their energy.

My dog Mead doesn't even need a dish for her food. For some reason, she likes to take her food out of the dish and put it on the floor. So, I'm pretty sure that she wouldn't mind at all if the food just started out there. Not surprisingly, the dogs are happy to take their water wherever they find it—although they seem to have a particular fondness for the toilet bowl.

You can be sure that my dogs also love rides in the car, opportunities to chase squirrels, long walks through the woods, and foot-twitching dreams. However, you can be just as sure that these things are luxuries and not requirements for their happy lives. They are quite happy, it appears, with a day in which they accomplish little more than spending some quality time with me, getting lots of rest, and taking a couple of leisurely trips to the yard to relieve themselves.

We humans, on the other hand, often make ourselves miserable by adding more and more complexity in our lives. When I was growing up my telephone number was a simple "Woodlawn 2281." Today when I ask for someone's telephone number, I will almost always get at least four different numbers. There's the work number, the home number, the cell phone number, and the fax number. Sometimes there's a pager number, too. In spite of all those ways to communicate, it seems that we as a culture have never been more profoundly out of touch with each other.

Our complex lives lead us toward more and more worry. No matter how much we accomplish we worry that it isn't enough. Before long, we find ourselves worrying about the fact that we worry so much.

My dogs—as far as I can tell—don't spend any time or effort worrying. If they have a problem they address it. If they have a dilemma, then they make a choice and resolve it. Sometimes when I go out and sit in the sun to read, I see that my dogs are confronted with a difficult decision. They like to be near me, but they also like to be in the shade. After all, sunbathing in a fur coat can't be all that pleasant. At first, the dogs choose companionship over comfort and come lie in the sun beside me. Then, when it gets too hot for them, they get up and move. They don't worry about what they should do, and they don't worry about changing their minds.

The ancient philosophers known as the Cynics had a great deal to teach us about living a simple life without worries. They believed that renouncing an all-out pursuit of luxury was the path to increased happiness. Diogenes, the most famous of all the Cynics, gloried in the simple life. Diogenes's home, for example, was nothing more than an old barrel. One day when he was sitting and enjoying the sun, Alexander the Great approached him and said, "I am the great King Alexander."

"I am Diogenes, the Cynic," was the reply.

"You can ask anything that you want of me, so what shall it be?" offered Alexander.

"I would like for you to stand out of my light," said Diogenes.

Alexander the Great reportedly said in response, "Had I not been Alexander, then I should have liked to have been Diogenes." It appears that even in Alexander the Great, we can detect a longing for a more simple life.

Two facts about the Cynics' approach to life are, I think, particularly noteworthy. One fact is that Diogenes and Alexander the Great died on the very same day in 323 B.C. Alexander the Great was thirty-three years old. Diogenes was ninety.

The other fact is that the word *cynic* in ancient Greek means "doglike." I invite you, dear reader, to make of these two facts whatever you wish.

"Patience is the companion of wisdom."

—ST. AUGUSTINE

DOGS ARE
PATIENT

My dogs have always loved to chase squirrels. In fact, they love to chase squirrels so much that we can't even use the *S*-word when we are at home. If we do, the dogs go berserk, running to every window checking for a sight of their favorite prey.

Once when we were out for a walk, my old standard poodle, Sweet Dreams, saw a squirrel in an open field. She took off in mad pursuit, but the squirrel made it safely to a single oak tree in the middle of the field. The squirrel went halfway up the tree and then turned and scolded Sweet Dreams severely. Sweetie realized, I suppose, that the squirrel had nowhere to go. So she decided to sit at the base of the tree and wait the squirrel out. I thought it was cute for a few minutes, and then I was ready to move on.

I tried everything to get her to continue our walk, but Sweetie was determined. She acted as if she and I had never been formally introduced. Finally, I tried something that I have seen parents do a thousand times. "Okay, so long Sweetie, you just stay right there, but I'm leaving." I was sure that by the time I was over the hill and out of sight, Sweetie would come running. I waited for at least five minutes and then trudged back up the hill. There she sat, patiently waiting at the base of the tree. She was staring at the squirrel.

I was tired of fooling around, so I gave Sweetie a scolding that was worse than anything the squirrel could muster. She briefly glanced at me with a look that said, "Get lost!" then returned her full attention to the squirrel. After all attempts at begging, persuading, and commanding failed, I finally went over and snapped on her leash. I tried to lead her away, but she dug in all four feet and let me know that she preferred a broken neck to surrendering her vigil beneath the tree. She gave me no option but to pick her up and carry her wiggling, resisting body all the way home.

I'm fully convinced that Sweet Dreams would have waited that squirrel out until one of the two of them keeled over from either starvation or exhaustion. That's the kind of patience that she had. In fact, all of my dogs have enormous patience. They know how to stop. They know how to wait. They seem to have certain wisdom and deep understanding about a truth that is very difficult for many of us: Things take time.

Many years back one of my college professors in philosophy first tried to teach me this valuable lesson. The first day of class he walked in and sat down at his desk in front of his eager students. He looked at us for what seemed to me to be an eternity without speaking. Then, slowly he took out his pipe and carefully filled the bowl with tobacco, still without a word to us. After he lit his pipe and took a few puffs, he looked at us and said, "Some things can't be hurried. The life of the mind takes time."

Our fast-paced, multitasking, and "right now" culture teaches us quite the opposite lesson. Everything from food to freeway must be swift, express, speedy, instant, rapid, quick, high-speed, and prompt. We can't tolerate the inconvenience of anything taking time. As the Danish philosopher Søren Kierkegaard observed, "Most men pursue pleasure with such haste, that they hurry past it."

Patience, as many great philosophers and spiritual teachers have taught, is a crucial human virtue. Aristotle, who probably wrote more than any of the early philosophers on the topic of virtue, taught that patience is a virtue that can be difficult and sometimes even bitter to practice. However, I believe that he was correct when he said that the practice of patience yields a fruit that is very sweet.

Sometimes all we need to taste that sweetness is to just sit under a tree and wait.

"The more I see of men, the more I admire dogs."

—Jeanne-Marie Roland

Dogs Know

When to Let Go

Celeste spotted the coyote a fraction of a second before I did. It was running smoothly along the crest of the hillside, a gray blur in the underbrush, and Celeste took off in hot pursuit before I could grab her.

"Celeste, no, stop!" I called out, horrified. A giant poodle, fresh from having her hair and nails done, madly tracking a wild coyote through the woods may sound amusing, but I was not amused. I was panic-stricken.

"Come back!" my wife screamed out. "Celeste, don't! Come here!"

But it was no use. Celeste had caught the coyote's scent, and nothing we could do could turn her back. I knew with a horrified certainty what was about to happen. I had heard stories about lone coyotes luring unsuspecting dogs into the woods. Packs of their wild brethren would be lying in wait to surround the defenseless house pets and tear them limb from limb.

"Celeste!" we screamed out together one last time, the panic rising in our voices. "Celeste, come back!" But Celeste was running even harder now, and she was gaining on the coyote, who must have outweighed her by twenty pounds. The coyote disappeared over the crest of the hill, and Celeste followed right behind, vanishing from sight.

We looked at each other, terrified. What could we do to save our dog's life? Our neighbor John King lived five minutes away over the next hill, and we ran, stumbling through the underbrush, to get his help. We banged on his front door and blurted out our story. "Into my truck!" he commanded, and pointed to his yellow pickup.

We jammed into the front seat of John's truck, and he gunned the four-wheel drive over the hill. We careened down the dirt road, turned around the bend to where we had last seen Celeste, and . . . there she was, waiting in the middle of the trail, panting heavily, tongue hanging out.

We leaped from the cab of the truck. Celeste ran over to us, tail wagging enthusiastically, and gave me a puzzled look, as if to say, "What happened to you two? I leave you alone for two minutes, and you completely disappear on me!" We greeted her with hugs and kisses, but after a few minutes of our tearful reunion, she shook herself all over and started loping back down the trail. She kept looking back over her shoulder at us as if to say, "What are you two stopping here for? Come on, let's go—did we come out here for a hike, or what?"

Dogs don't dwell on the past. They know when to let go of things. Now that the coyote was gone, it was gone. There was no need for Celeste to be frightened about it, to worry about it, to endlessly relive the experience. What was the point of continuing to think about it?

When something goes wrong, those of us with two legs often love to talk about it and think about it. Somehow we wind up staying stuck in the troubled past, instead of moving on to the untroubled present. My wife and I would have remained standing right where we were, analyzing what had happened with the coyote over and over again.

We had completely forgotten about continuing the hike. But Celeste wasn't having any of that. Something a lot more interesting was probably waiting around the next bend in the path. It was time to move on!

"A dog teaches a boy fidelity, perseverance, and to turn around three times before lying down."

—ROBERT BENCHLEY

DOGS KNOW HOW TO GET COMFORTABLE

I am always disturbing my dogs' peace and calm. I don't really do it on purpose, but it is as predictable as sunrise. Like most people's dogs my dogs just can't seem to bear being in a different room from me. So, every time that I change rooms, the dogs feel obliged to do the same.

I used to feel responsible for unsettling them, especially when I was going to be returning very shortly to exactly the same spot that I had just vacated. So, I tried to explain that they didn't need to move, since I would be right back. I have come to the conclusion that they understood; it's just that— even if I was only going for five minutes—they wanted to move with me. I think that the reason that dogs don't mind being bothered is that it is very easy for them to get comfortable all over again.

My dogs have shown that they can get comfortable very quickly in virtually any situation. Three big dogs take up lots of room in my car, but they know how to work it out without bumping into each other. When I go out on the patio, they each have their favorite patio chair. Although they are each bigger than their respective chairs, they know how to curl up into a convenient ball so that they fit just right. If I decide to move into the living room, then it's no big deal at all. They each have a cozy spot there, too.

All my moving from place to place is not a big disturbance to my dogs because they are very willing to participate in the ongoing process of change. The reason it is so easy for them is that they quite naturally and effortlessly maintain a balance and harmony of mind, body, and spirit. We might say that dogs are centered, which is simply the ability to stay interested and involved in the experience of the present moment.

Some years back I enrolled in a Tai Chi class that was taught on the beach. Our teacher said that we should seek to become so light and comfortable with the movement of our bodies that we would leave no footprints in the sand. The Tai Chi movements, he said, are physical, but the real emphasis of the practice is mental. The practice of Tai Chi is a meditative one that helps the student to concentrate and to cultivate an understanding of change—in all its aspects—as a natural part of the life process.

I remember my teacher remarking one day, "Children and dogs are already Tai Chi masters." He invited us to watch how dogs have the capacity to be active without any tension and how they are fully occupied in the present moment both when moving and at rest. This is why comfort comes so easily to them.

We can achieve the same kind of simple comfort in our own lives. However, we must first turn away from the idea that comfort is something that can be achieved through manipulating the external environment. Real comfort cannot be achieved in our lives by spending more money, making our material surroundings more luxurious, or—for that matter—by finding ways to distract ourselves from our discomfort. These approaches can only briefly and unsuccessfully mask our true situation.

The only way to achieve permanent and lasting comfort is to become centered within ourselves. Genuine comfort, in the final analysis, is an inside job.

"If your dog is fat, then you aren't getting enough exercise."

—AUTHOR UNKNOWN

DOGS ARE IN TUNE WITH THEIR BODIES

Celeste and Mead are much younger than Blue. When I throw the ball, the two young ones chase after it at breakneck speed. They both seem to love the competition. Sometimes I still urge Blue to join them in the chase. "Get the ball, Blue!" I yell, but she is very satisfied to trot slowly a few paces in that direction and then watch over the younger girls.

Years ago she would run through a wall to be first to get the ball. One time Kim Verbois, a friend of mine who is a dog trainer of hunting retrievers, invited me to join her at the lake near my house. She was working her champion field retriever, a male golden. I never did any field training with Blue. Blue's father, however, was a national field-retrieving champion, and I think Kim wanted to see if Blue had "the right stuff."

Kim threw the bumper far out in the lake and then sent both dogs on the retrieve. The first time that Blue returned with the bumper, Kim remarked, "Isn't it interesting the way Chaz let the female win?" After ten more tosses and ten more times of Blue dropping the bumper at her feet, Kim had a different view. "Give it up, Chaz," she told her dog, "this girl is way too fast and strong for you."

As I look at her now, with her muzzle turning white and at least fifteen more pounds of girth, she rests comfortably in total harmony with who she is. This same dog, who used to run ultradistances with ease, now struggles on our morning five-mile run. The other dogs run ahead and dash here and there off the trail, investigating every curiosity. Blue is happy to run at my side, occasionally mixing in a walk break, before jogging to catch up.

I'm struck by the fact that she has so easily, naturally, and gracefully accepted the changes in her body. She is just as happy and at home in her body as she has ever been. In fact, her transition from a young pup to an old dog has been so smooth and carefree that I barely noticed. It is as if I woke up one morning and realized, "Blue is getting old."

Never in the history of humanity has the body been more of a problem than it is at present. Both men and women are fixated on issues of the body. Obesity is at an all-time high. Eating disorders are the order of the day. These disorders are not really about food and weight. They are symptoms of something much deeper going on in the human psyche. We are using food to stuff down our uncomfortable feelings, regardless of the consequences to our spiritual, physical, and emotional health.

I do not want to trivialize or oversimplify a problem with such deep psychological, emotional, and spiritual roots. However, I think we would do well to find some new ideals and role models when it comes to our bodies. The media and entertainment images that fascinate us are, in reality, nothing more than that—images. Even the most lean, skeletal super-models and movie stars get airbrush treatments to their photos. Muscled men with ripped abdomens achieve the look with diet, harmful drugs, and exercise techniques that one could hardly call "natural."

Rather than the mirages and fantasies that currently inspire us, we could perhaps find our inspiration in role models that demonstrate perfect confidence, harmony, and comfort with their bodies. Certainly we could learn something useful if we would turn our gaze toward those among us who enjoy and accept their bodies as they are and who know how to age with grace—our dogs.

*"If you get to thinking that you are a person
of some influence, try ordering
someone else's dog around."*

—WILL ROGERS

DOGS DON'T
ROLL OVER FOR
JUST ANYONE

The first time that I ever saw Lucy, she was exhausted. She was lounging under a tree in the Sierra Nevada mountains with her friend and companion Larry King. Larry was out on the trail training for the Western States Endurance Run, a one-hundred-mile footrace on rugged trails from Squaw Valley to Auburn, California. I was training for the same race and happened across Lucy and Larry while on a thirty-mile training run.

I have done some ultradistance running with my own dogs before. Blue once ran forty miles with me and was ready for even more. I've also known other runners who took their dogs with them on very long runs. However, the dogs were usually Labs, goldens, or some kind of hound. I was a little surprised to see Larry out with Lucy, a one-hundred-pound English sheepdog.

Larry explained that Lucy had tired after twenty-five miles and was refusing to budge. He said that he was probably going to have to carry her down the mountain the last five miles. I joined them for the last leg of the run. I wasn't going to miss the chance to see a man try to run with a huge dog draped over his shoulders. I discovered that Larry was a strong and determined fellow because he was able to carry Lucy down the mountain trail. In addition, several weeks later he finished the hundred-mile endurance run on what I am sure was less training than virtually any other runner in the race.

Larry and I became fast friends as we covered the last five miles together that day. Afterward he told me that he and Lucy had a condo in Tahoe City, and he invited me to stay with them for the weeks leading up to the race. That's how Larry and I became training partners and how Lucy and I became roommates.

Lucy worshipped Larry, and the feeling was mutual.

Larry pampered Lucy as much as any man has ever pampered a dog. Whenever we stopped at a restaurant, he would order a fine meal for Lucy and take it to her in the car, so she could eat while we were eating. He referred to his flashy BMW as "Lucy's doghouse." She went virtually everywhere with Larry. She did not, however, join us on any more long training runs. Larry left her with plenty of water beside the car with a simple, "Stay Lucy! We will be back." He would leave the back door open just in case she wanted to get into her house. We would run on the trail for five or six hours, and when we returned Lucy would be waiting patiently just as Larry had asked her to do.

Lucy was, in fact, one of the best-behaved dogs that I have ever known; that is, if Larry was doing the asking. In the several weeks that we were roommates, I never saw her refuse to do anything Larry asked of her. On the other hand, if I made even the simplest request, it was more like I was talking to a sheep than a sheepdog. Lucy became suddenly blind and deaf whenever I had a request of her. She was the embodiment of the old Biblical wisdom, "You cannot serve two masters."

If we humans could understand this simple wisdom as well as Lucy did, then I believe that we would be much happier in the long run. In truth, so many of us end up giving ourselves over to masters that—in our hearts—we really don't want to follow. Our lives get consumed with doing what we think that we should do, instead of what we really want to do. I once had a conversation with the influential American psychologist Albert Ellis. He said, "You know, people get so caught up in doing what they think they should do that they end up *shoulding* all over themselves."

Life is far too short to waste even a day pursuing things that we don't really care about. Perhaps one of the most helpful questions that we could ask ourselves—both early in our lives and often—is "for whom or what am I willing to roll over?" The almighty dollar is usually the "master" for whom we are most willing to roll over, of course. I meet many people who aren't doing what they would really like to do with their lives because of concerns about money. However, when we sacrifice our passion, we have a good chance of ending up miserable.

Joseph Campbell offered some wonderful advice about which master to select. He said simply, "Follow your bliss." If we want to have all the delight, joy, and satisfaction available to us in life, then we must find out what we really love, and then give it our all.

It's helpful to remember that happiness is not something that just happens to us. Happiness is something that is achieved. One of the surest ways to achieve it is to find out what truly enchants us and then focus on it with Lucylike devotion.

"One of the problems with humans that I see is that they aren't so good at finding things that they bury."

—CONVERSATIONS WITH DOG

DOGS SCRATCH WHERE IT ITCHES

There is a minor controversy about the role that Sigmund Freud's Chow Chow dog, Jo-Fi, actually played in the renowned psychologist's work with his clients. Some have claimed that Freud depended heavily upon Jo-Fi for help with his patients. They say that his dog attended all his sessions and that Freud made psychological judgments about the patient based upon how close or far away from the patient Jo-Fi would curl up and lie down for the hour. They even claim that Jo-Fi would "announce" to Freud the end of each session by getting up and walking over to the door. Others claim that this is pure, unadulterated dog poop.

There is near universal agreement, however, that if Freud's work had been about analyzing dogs instead of people, then he would have had to find another job. He would have suffered, no doubt, from "employment envy."

Dogs are not good candidates for psychoanalysis. When dogs have a problem, like an irritating flea, for example, they address the problem in a straightforward, head-on manner. If it itches, then they scratch it. My dogs are so adroit with teeth and toes that they contort their bodies and scratch virtually any part of their itching anatomy before you can say, "Call Freud!"

Imagine what it would be like if our dogs used the classic Freudian defense mechanisms when they had problems. I have a difficult time thinking of my dogs defending their egos with these standard human defenses. What would it be like if Blue had a flea, but she was stuck in denial? "Flea? What Flea? I don't have a flea! Why in heavens name would I even consider scratching? Nothing itches!"

My old poodle, Sweet Dreams, was as sweet as her name suggests. However, she really had it in for our letter carrier. I guess if Sweet Dreams was using the defense of projection, her thoughts upon seeing the postman would be, "I'm not the one who hates the letter carrier! Blue hates the letter carrier! Actually, I sort of like him, what with his big bag and all."

Or, what about Celeste? I can imagine her heavily into rationalization. "Yes, I admit that I dug those very nice holes in the garden. My motivation, of course, was to save my mom the problem of digging when she gets ready to plant those geraniums."

No, dogs do not confront their problems by defending their egos. Many of us, however, when confronted with emotional suffering in our lives don't want to act like our dogs and go straight after the problem. Rather than dealing directly with our suffering, we try to ignore it and avoid it in a variety of ways.

The Danish philosopher Søren Kierkegaard, who wrote much about the human problem of despair, said that rather than address our despair we choose to "tranquilize ourselves with the trivial." So we drink, we overeat, we take drugs, we watch television, we shop, or we find other ways to avoid the issue. We will do almost anything but deal directly with our pain and suffering. But time after time this approach fails and leads us to even more suffering because these solutions provide only superficial, quick fixes that don't really resolve the issue. We have a much better chance of achieving a life of happiness if we stop avoiding the psychological problems that all of us are sure to have. Rather, we can learn to face our problems head-on.

In short, if it itches, then scratch it.

*"If a dog will not come to you after having
looked you in the face, you should go
home and examine your conscience."*
—WOODROW WILSON

DOGS ARE
GOOD JUDGES OF
CHARACTER

You won't likely meet a better-hearted person than my wife. Most people sense it just by looking at her. Her gentle, kind, and calm presence radiates from her being. Dogs sense it instantly.

Not long ago she and I were on the way to the symphony in our temporary home in Guanajuato, Mexico. We were both very excited about hearing the symphony, but just as excited about getting our first look inside the marvelous *Teatro Juarez*.

We stopped on the way to watch a street mime entertaining a large crowd a few blocks from the *Teatro*. I was lost in the comedy, so I didn't notice—at first—that my wife had slipped away from the crowd. When I turned around, I saw her down on her knees on the cobblestone street holding the head of a razor-thin, mange-ridden, German shepherd. The dog looked to be no more than about five months old.

When I arrived at her side, she looked up and said, "We have to help this dog! She found me. She's starving."

I tried to resist. "What's so different about *this* starving dog?" I said to myself. I thought about the hundreds of other stray dogs that we had seen on the Guanajuato streets. What made this one so different?

"What about the symphony?" was all I could weakly manage.

"Forget the symphony," I was told. "Go find some rope for a leash."

I went to several nearby shops searching for something that could serve as a leash. After a fruitless search, I found my wife sitting on the sidewalk with the pup's head in her lap. She was stroking the dog's head and assuring her that everything would be fine.

When my wife saw that I had returned empty-handed, she directed me to take the laces out of my shoes. "Tie them together and make a leash," she urged. But the shoelace leash proved worthless because the dog was too weak to walk. So I picked her up and carried her the half mile back to our house.

We fed her small amounts of food every three hours for the remainder of the night. I have never seen a dog eat with such passion and gratitude. Between feedings she slept comfortably—I imagined for the first time in her young life—on a blanket beside our bed. Our dogs must have sensed her vulnerability for they were curious but gave her plenty of space.

The next morning we took the dog to the vet. We were told that after a few days of rest and some medication for the mange, she should be fine. She would need to be quarantined for the next five days, so as not to spread the mange. The vet also discovered a broken leg that had healed improperly, so she always would have a limp.

This vet had a great record for placing dogs that had been rescued from the streets. He told us that he thought he could find a good home for the dog. We assured the vet that if he couldn't find the perfect home for her, then we would keep her. We told him that we weren't sure exactly how, but we would take the dog back to the United States.

The following week the vet called to tell us that the dog was doing very well and that he had found her a wonderful new home. After being assured by the vet that the dog would be spayed, we gave our blessing to the adoption.

As I reflected on the whole experience, the one thing that struck me most about it was my wife's insistence that this dog had found her, not the other way around. I have no doubt that my wife is right. Dogs have an absolutely brilliant sense about people. I have no idea how they do it, but dogs can size up a person's character with a few quick sniffs and a deep look into their eyes. This dog was desperate, so she sized up the entire crowd and then made the selection that she knew would save her life.

I believe that—on the whole—dogs generally are looking for something good in the people that they meet. In fact, they sometimes see good qualities in people that those same people have not yet realized in themselves. I do my very best to keep an open mind; however, I must admit that on those rare occasions that my dogs take a disliking to someone, I pay attention. When I don't particularly like someone that my dogs find to be wonderful, I am more likely to question my judgment than theirs.

A friend recently told me that both she and her daughter's dog despised the guy that her daughter was dating. Dog and mother were allied in their contempt for the man; however, her daughter was deeply enamored. When the guy turned out to be a first-class jerk, my friend extracted a promise from her daughter. "I know you'll never listen to my opinion about your boyfriends, but swear to me that from now on you'll listen to the dog!"

Perhaps in our distant animal past, we humans had a better capacity to size up others quickly, but as moderns we have lost the capacity. I know that my dogs seem to be much better judges of character than I am. Unlike my dogs, my first impressions and perceptions are often wrong. I form instant judgments of other people and I have a hard time letting go of them.

When dogs don't like someone, they have the good sense to stay away from him or her. On the other hand, when they need people to share their love, they find them. Seek out the good and take care to avoid the bad is the way a dog lives out his day. Not a bad way, I say, to approach life.

"Don't sweat the small stuff
and it's all small stuff."

—POPULARIZED BY RICHARD CARLSON

DOGS DON'T
SWEAT THE
SMALL STUFF
(OR ANYTHING ELSE!)

My dogs always have been working dogs. They actually have two jobs. In addition to their part-time work in the home security business, they have full-time jobs as my running companions. I love to jog for long distances, and my dogs' enthusiasm for their work as my running partners is near boundless.

Even when the heat is oppressive, the dogs always want to go. I try to reason with them and tell them that running in a fur coat won't be much fun in the heat, but they will hear none of it. When I first tell them that they have to stay at home because it is too hot, they collapse in disappointment and despair by the door. In the past, when I tried to jog away while convincing myself that I was doing what was in their best interests, they pressed their noses to the window and looked at me with such pity-evoking stares that I knew that my run would be ruined by guilt.

My daily run is one of the most joyful and peaceful parts of my day, and I didn't like having it turned into a guilt trip. So, we reached a compromise. The dogs must take a quick, cooling dip in the swimming pool before we leave. For my golden retriever this is a bit like inviting Br'er Rabbit for a stroll in the briar patch. For my poodle, on the other hand, who likes to touch water only on her own terms, it is a sacrifice. This is a sacrifice, however, that she is willing to make to avoid being left behind.

On our hot runs, every water fountain and yard sprinkler provides another opportunity to wet down the dogs' coats so that they can stay reasonably cool. The look of the water-soaked dogs elicits friendly comments from passersby like, "Somebody has been in the water!" or "Looks as though someone has been for a swim!" Recently, however, I overheard a comment that made my blood boil.

We had only been running for about a half of a mile

when I overheard an observation that was made by a thirty-something woman who was in the park with her young daughter of about six. I'm not sure if it was intended that I hear the comment or not. The remark was directed at the daughter, but it was not whispered, and I thought that I was the intended audience. "Oh look, Allie, at how those dogs are sweating! Poor things. I can't believe that man is making them run in all this heat!"

I pretended that I didn't hear as I ran on by; however, my ears were burning, and I was incensed. *How dare she!* I thought, *She has no idea what she is talking about.* As I continued my run, I was totally lost in negative fantasy about all the things that I should have said to her. I continued to rehearse and modify my responses as the run continued.

All my angry, fantasized responses were variations on the same theme: "You know it's bad enough that you are so profoundly ignorant, but even worse, you are passing your monumental stupidity on to the next generation! I am not MAKING these dogs run and furthermore, you peabrain, DOGS DON'T SWEAT! That's why they're always panting! That's why their tongues are always hanging out!" As the miles rolled by, I refined my attack, changed words here and there, but couldn't stop reliving the experience.

With about a mile to go to get back to my house, I stopped for the last time to wet the dogs down at one of the fountains in the park. As I poured water over their heads and necks, I noticed that they were both smiling.

Whereas I had managed to make myself miserable for the last hour, they simply loved their run. Unlike my dogs, I had allowed myself to spoil my own experience. I had taken some really small stuff and blown it so far out of proportion that my run had been one giant emotional sweat. The dogs weren't sweating anything.

The last mile of my run was very pleasant. Once again, I was able to smile as I remembered that life is far too short to spend it stuck in the negative. My life is so much happier when I don't sweat the small stuff. When we find ourselves fretting and concerned about insignificant things in our lives, maybe we can ask ourselves this question: "Would my dog sweat this?" The answer can serve as a gentle reminder. "Dogs don't sweat anything!"

"The supreme accomplishment is to blur the line between work and play."

—ARNOLD TOYNBEE

DOGS TURN WORK INTO PLAY

Whenever I hear someone complaining, "My boss is working me like a dog," I simply ask the question, "Oh, really? Have you ever taken a moment to notice how your dog actually DOES spend her day? Today would be your lucky day if you were working like your dog!"

Dogs don't make a distinction between work and play. Everything is fun to them, and every situation is a new one, full of infinite possibilities for joy and connection. We humans surely would be more successful in our jobs if we approached our work with the enthusiasm, dedication, sensitivity, and the wonderful attitude toward life in general of a good working dog.

Of course I'll be the first to admit that sometimes dogs can bring too much playfulness to the job. Several years ago, I hired a young man to build a new deck in my backyard. He told me he would have it finished in a couple of days. I hoped that he could because I had agreed to pay him by the hour. I like to think my dog, Blue, is a good watchdog, so I left her in the backyard to keep an eye on him. When I returned many hours later, he had hardly made any progress at all on the deck. The worker explained that he was unable to accomplish much because Blue kept bringing him the ball to throw. He said, "Every time I tried to stop playing, she wouldn't stop barking until I threw the ball again. She wore me out. Maybe tomorrow you can leave the dog inside, so I can get some work done!"

So, maybe we don't want to play so much that we accomplish nothing. On the other hand, when we can "blur the distinction between work and play" we are much more productive.

The wonderful weimaraners that appear in the photographs, paintings, drawings, and videos of William Wegman are good examples of working dogs who have fun on the job.

Wegman dresses his dogs in all sorts of outrageous costumes, which invariably bring a laugh. He says the dogs "see it as an interactive game. The more serious the endeavor the more they thrive on it and, despite my silly photographs, it's serious work for the dogs and they take it very seriously." Wegman's dogs are masters of the approach that we all need to take with our work, whether that work is in the office, at home, in the classroom, or anywhere else. They take their work seriously, but they take themselves lightly by seeing work as a game.

Just like Wegman's dogs, we need to learn that play and work are not contradictory ideas. If we are going to be happy at work—which is the place where most of us spend the majority of our waking hours—then we must learn to integrate work and play. How can we make this happen? There are many creative ways to use laughter and play to bring more happiness into our lives at work.

At the MasterCard call center in St. Louis, for example, the administration showed that it is not just dogs that can be dressed up in silly outfits. They declared one day to be "Dress Up Your Supervisor Day!" All supervisors agreed to be dressed up for the day by the people who reported to them. There were a few simple ground rules: no cross-gender dressing and not too much skin showing. But a visitor to the facility that day would have noticed that Elvis was definitely in the building, along with an assortment of nuns and biker chicks roaming the halls!

Jeanne Anderson, who is director of Insurance Processing at the Farm Credit Services of America, tried her own variation of the dress-up idea. "Our headquarters moved across town this weekend, and Thursday was the big moving day," recounts Jeanne. "I told our team to dress me up however they wanted for moving day. The only stipulation was that it would not offend our CEO.

"They chose to dress me up as a mime, so I couldn't talk for the whole day. What a hoot! This was not a random choice—I am known as a rather verbose person. It cost nothing, took very little time, and provided fun for not only our team, but the entire office staff—plus the movers!"

Working like your dog is especially important in the high-pressure world of business, where we seem to take ourselves far too seriously. As our dogs eagerly remind us, work can be fun!

"Is not giving a need? Is not receiving mercy?"

—FRIEDRICH NIETZSCHE

DOGS KNOW HOW
TO RECEIVE
GIFTS

Celeste is allergic to so many foods that she can no longer have a dog biscuit for her evening treat. Instead, she has a rice cake. But Celeste is just as excited as she can be about her ritual evening gift. Her joyful anticipation of her nightly snack makes it fun for both of us. I hold the rice cake up in the air and Celeste sits and looks longingly at her treat. Then, she shifts her gaze to stare into my eyes, as if to say, "Enough of this dog training already—let's have it!"

As soon as I say, "Take it!" she leaps into the air and grabs it out of my hand and prances over to her dog bed. She prolongs her evening treat longer than I could believe possible by daintily gnawing at it bit by tiny bit. She obviously enjoys the gift, and shows her appreciation by wagging her tail enthusiastically when I walk over and ask her how she likes it.

I don't know if it is actually "better to give than to receive," but I do know that giving is a lot easier than receiving for some people. There is a certain vulnerability involved in truly receiving a gift fully and in letting in the gesture of love that accompanies it. When Celeste is chomping on her rice cake, she's not thinking, "I don't deserve this," or "You shouldn't have," or "This is not really what I wanted," or "This is so embarrassing," or "Now I have to get something for you." Her entire being radiates, "This is great! Just what I needed! How thoughtful of you!" Her enthusiastic acceptance of whatever gifts I have to share makes me feel wonderful about being able to provide these little presents for her.

One of the things that many great spiritual teachers have taught is that if we can only take from others and are unable to give, then we are failing to love. On the other hand, if we are able only to give and not receive, then we are probably using our giving merely as a way to try to control other people. True happiness, they say, comes through finding a balance between giving and receiving.

When we learn to both give and receive gifts with no strings attached, as if it were the most natural thing in the world, then we get to discover an even deeper gift—the gift of love that comes along with being in a relationship with those we care about.

"Dig under fence—Why? Because it's there. Because it's there. Because it's there."

—AUTHOR UNKNOWN

DOGS LOOK BENEATH THE SURFACE

People sometimes ask me why dogs dig. I'm no expert in animal behavior, but to me it seems fairly obvious. They have their reasons. Humans often have different reasons for the same behavior, and I think dogs are like us in that respect.

When a dog digs on a hot day, I figure that she is trying to fix up a nice, cool place to have a comfortable nap. Dogs have great senses, so I'm sure they dig sometimes because they smell or hear something beneath the ground. At other times they dig because they are motivated by the desire to escape captivity.

When Blue was pregnant she dug several times, and I'm convinced that she was instinctively building a nest. Plenty of times dogs dig because they want to bury something or dig something up. I think that dogs most often dig because they are just looking for something to keep them entertained. I'll bet when you've been bored you have, at times, done stranger things than digging a hole.

If I must generalize, then, dogs dig because there is something below the surface that holds some interest for them. I think that's a great reason for us to dig, too. I think digging is a fine metaphor for what we need to do if we want to be happy. We speak of "finding happiness," and I think that makes good sense, if we know the right places to look. I think finding happiness requires a search, and I'm fairly certain we aren't going to find it on the surface.

Back in college I had a philosophy professor named Ben Petty for a course in nineteenth-century philosophy. He used to hold up his dog-eared copy of some nearly unfathomable work like Kant's *Prolegomena to Any Future Metaphysics* and earnestly say to us as he slapped the text, "There's a lot of gold in these pages, but remember you've got to dig beneath the surface if you expect to find gold!"

In our culture so much of our life is spent focused on the

surface, that we have little time for digging for the gold that is within each one of us. Our culture places so much emphasis upon the shallow exterior where "image is everything" (as a popular commercial told us not long ago), that we get distracted from the important interior search. Yet a search for the right "image" will provide us only with fool's gold.

The 1995 Nobel Laureate, Seamus Heaney, has a poem called "Digging." He writes about his father and grandfather, who as farmers literally dug in the earth for their livelihoods. Heaney shows us, however, that there are many ways that we can dig for happiness. Heaney does his digging with his pen, rather than the spade of his forefathers.

If we want to find all the happiness that life can offer, then—in whatever way we can—each of us must dig for what lies buried within our souls. The great Greek philosopher, Socrates, warned us of caring too much for those things that glitter on the surface—money, fame, prestige, and all those other things that keep us from the task of digging. His famous maxim, "the life unexamined is not worth living," challenges us to put nurturing our soul before those other things.

This is not to suggest that we cannot enjoy the material world. Socrates had a great sense of humor. He loved a good party and lively dialogue. The point that Socrates made was if we are to truly enjoy anything in life, then it will be as a result of coming to deep self-understanding.

Our dogs have all sorts of reasons to dig for all sorts of things. So do we. We dig so that we can uncover the precious jewel that is our true self.

LESSON 42

"I can't get no satisfaction."
—MICK JAGGER

DOGS ARE
SATISFIED

Dogs are virtually always deeply satisfied. I think if my dogs have a mantra then it might be, "This is good enough." My dogs love long runs in the woods, off the leash. However, when all they get is a short walk through the city, they are satisfied—it's good enough.

I am certain that they love the fact that I often fix them very special meals, but when they get dry food from a sack, they are still satisfied—it's good enough. They love to sleep on the couch or a comfy chair in the air-conditioned house, but if I put them outside on the concrete patio, they are comfortable—it's good enough.

I believe that one of the main reasons my dogs stay so happy and satisfied with their lives is that they always live fully in the present moment. They don't compare their current experience to past experiences. They are totally committed to life in the here and now.

When Blue rolls on her back in the grass, she is right there for the experience. When Mead chases a squirrel, she is not thinking about what she might be doing later. When Celeste grabs a stick and struts around proudly while the other dogs try unsuccessfully to take it away, she is not contemplating what else she might be doing. The dogs are totally involved in being alive in the moment. They aren't constantly analyzing each moment or projecting themselves into the past or the future. I'm sure that if they could tell us, they would say, "Life is good. This is sufficient. I'm satisfied."

Many of us feel an emptiness and a lack of fulfillment in our lives, regardless of how much we have or get. We go around searching for something that will make our lives beautiful and complete. However, nothing we find really nourishes us, and we remain dissatisfied.

We could experience so much more satisfaction with life by paying more attention to the present moment. Every moment presents us with the opportunity to experience our lives fully—we are always surrounded by the richness of the world. It is always there for us if we are there for it. There is no better get-rich-quick scheme than that of learning to live in the present moment.

I know that I sometimes catch myself thinking about what I am going to have for supper, while I am eating my lunch! How will I ever get the full satisfaction that my lunch can offer if I am not there for it? If I am thinking about the next meal or, for that matter, anything but my lunch, then I can't be fully present for my meal.

I can't imagine my dogs thinking about their next meal while they're eating this one. They are too all-consumed in loving the meal they are having right now. The same is true of everything that they do. But this ability to be "in the now" is certainly not limited to our dogs. We can develop this same kind of awareness of being present for our life as it moves from moment to moment.

How wonderful that we have the opportunity to be as satisfied as our dogs. Life is there for the taking, you lucky dog!

*"Of all the things I miss from veterinary practice,
puppy breath is one of the most fond memories."*
—Dr. Tom Cat

DOGS DON'T
CARE ABOUT DOG
BREATH

Right up there alongside hot popped corn, fresh rain on a dusty road, gardenias, and high mountain cedar, you will find puppy breath in my personal "Best Smells Hall of Fame." Several years ago, when Blue had puppies, I couldn't get enough of scratching the sides of their little mouths in order to induce a yawn and then poking my nose inside for a giant whiff of gloriously smelling puppy breath.

Unfortunately, this delightful odor lasts only about seven or eight weeks. After that, puppy breath becomes dog breath faster than you can say, "What disgusting thing has that dog got in her mouth now?" Dogs are connoisseurs of foul tastes and odors. I can't think of a single disgusting thing that my dogs are not willing to put in their mouths. It shows on their breath.

Dogs have, of course, an incredible sense of smell. They have between 125 and 225 million sensory cell receptors in their noses. In comparison, their human companions have between 5 and 15 million. Their noses are so rich in blood vessels, nerve endings, and receptor cells that some researchers have estimated that dogs' sense of smell is about a million times better than ours. Their sense of smell is so complex that it is said that they can smell all the various ingredients of a pizza at once!

One day I was running with Blue on the trail that runs alongside the Willamette River. Suddenly, she jerked at her leash and pulled me sharply to the side into the grass. I took this as a sign that she needed to make an emergency "pit stop." However, she just kept pulling and lugged me over to a half-eaten chicken leg. She had picked up the scent at a full trot from fifteen feet away!

This, of course, is why working dogs are used to sniff out drugs, bombs, fires, and who knows what else. Given this extra-ordinary sense of smell, it is a bit difficult to understand why they must put their noses all the way up another dog's rear end in order to get the sensory information that they obviously need so desperately. The same is true when they investigate great "finds" in the yard, even when what they have found is what they heretofore have left! If I have seen it once I have seen it a thousand times: one of my dogs walks over to a pile of dog poop, delicately lifts one paw, leans down to a distance of one millimeter, and takes several giant whiffs.

So, it's obvious that many things that we think smell great—like perhaps fried chicken—our dogs also think smell good, and from fifteen feet away, at that. On the other hand, there are things that we think smell horrible from fifteen feet, which they don't mind at all, even at close range. My own conclusion is that our attitude toward smell is much more cultural and psychological than biological.

The subjective, cultural nature of smell is supported even further by the fact that some things smell bad to people of one culture but good to people of another culture. Of course, there are also differences in preference from person to person within the same culture.

It seems to me that in this culture we have become obsessed with covering up our natural body odors. I once had a relationship with a woman who insisted that she brush her teeth and gargle before I could give her a good-morning kiss. The only problem was that then she no longer smelled like a person. Her mouth smelled and tasted like a freshly disinfected sink.

Our need to cover our authentic smell is deeply rooted in our psychology—a mind-set that has us convinced that being an animal is not such a good thing. Body smells are animal smells, so if we can disguise the fact that we have the smell of animals then we can disguise also the undeniable fact that we are animals. After all, isn't the whole evolution of manners a direct result of trying to distinguish us from animals? Many times as a child I heard, "You're as dirty as a dog!" and "You're as sloppy as a pig!"

Why will accepting our own animal nature and the natural odors that go with it make us any happier? In short, as many philosophers and psychologists have suggested, we are unique in the animal kingdom. We are beasts, but we are also angels. We have awareness of our own vulnerability and mortality. If we cannot accept both our animal and angel natures, then we cannot be truly happy.

Nature is not our enemy. A lack of awareness is a much greater threat to our happiness than an occasional whiff of who we really are.

*"I lie belly-up
In the Sunshine, happier than
You will ever be."*

—AUTHOR UNKNOWN

DOGS ARE
OPTIMISTIC

One of the things that keeps dogs happier than many of their human companions is that they seem to have an innate optimism about life. A good example of this is the difference we find between dogs and humans when it comes to riding in cars.

Recent research shows that we spend considerably more time in our cars each year. Even those of us who don't live in big cities often spend hours every week behind the wheel. Those of us who live in large cities are now estimated to spend an additional forty-hour week in our car each year compared to what we did a decade ago. Incidents of road rage are increasing all the time. No wonder we're angry—we've just lost a week out of our lives to sitting in traffic!

We humans tend to get into our cars with a certain grim determination. We start our engines with our moods already set for pessimism. In just the past few days, I have observed several incidents in traffic where very minor and not dangerous driving errors have induced fits of wild screaming and angry gesturing on the part of other drivers who were only slightly inconvenienced. Someone driving too slowly in the fast lane, or someone cutting them off as they change lanes can send another driver into a crazed state of swearing and fist shaking. It seems to be acceptable driving behavior to bark at other drivers and get ready to bite off their heads with the least provocation.

Surely, this is not good for our happiness or our health

Imagine how wonderful it would be if we could remember to view our time in the car the same way as our dogs approach their car rides. Day after day, my dogs get in the car with wild enthusiasm. Whenever they hear the jingle of my car keys, the dogs start running in circles with uninhibited eagerness. Blue and Celeste love going for rides, and they couldn't care less, it appears, where we are going. To them, every ride is a joy ride. They eagerly poke their heads out the window. Their noses twitch as they sniff the air for olfactory mysteries that I will never understand. As the rushing wind blows their ears back at a forty-five degree angle, they are pictures of true happiness.

I heard someone say recently that there are three keys to living a really happy life—attitude, attitude, and attitude. So much of our attitude is determined by what we believe. All of us have heard the old saying that "seeing is believing." However, the reverse of that is also true. Our expectations and beliefs about things will influence greatly what actually happens in our lives.

If we wake up, for example, very optimistic and cheerful about the day and believe that it is going to be a grand day, then we greatly enhance the likelihood that this is just the kind of day that we will find. On the other hand, if we look at the day with a sense of pessimistic dread, then our beliefs may well play a role in creating an awful day.

Think how different my life could be if I could view my time in the car with the same optimism as my dogs. I can see myself now running around in circles with enormous enthusiasm as I grab for my keys. I picture myself cocking my head slightly and sniffing the fresh morning air as I leap into the driver's seat. Occasionally, I roll down the window and poke my head into the wind and notice the puffs of air through my hair. Each time that I get stopped in traffic, I see that I have an opportunity to stick my head out the window and flash a big, toothy smile at everyone around. If I can just remember to ride like my dog, then my car will be transformed into an island of deep and abiding joy.

Undoubtedly, I will be soon faced with backed-up traffic and careless or rude drivers who have not yet discovered the wisdom of riding like our dogs. I will look at them sorrowfully as they bark and bite the heads off other travelers. They may even bark at me, but I won't bark back. I'll be too busy smiling and wagging my tail.

*"In order to really enjoy a dog, one doesn't
merely try to train him to be semihuman.
The point of it is to open oneself to the
possibility of becoming partly a dog."*

—EDWARD HOAGLAND

DOGS KNOW
THEIR LIMITS

My dogs love to go camping. We have fitted out little backpacks for Blue and Celeste, and they seem to take great delight in carrying some of their own supplies on their backs. Sometimes they'll walk alongside us, but more often than not they'll run up ahead, turning around and doubling back to keep us in view whenever they get too far ahead on the trail. Occasionally the two of them will spot a deer, and, ignoring our shouted instructions to stay on the trail, they'll go crashing through the underbrush in hot pursuit of a leaping stag they can't possibly catch. Ten minutes later they'll be back, tongues hanging out and tails wagging from the fun of it all.

Whenever we come to a river that's rushing too fast to be forded or a bridge that's missing some of its planks, Blue and Celeste will be waiting patiently for us to catch up to them and help them figure out how to proceed. One thing I've noticed about them, especially in the woods, is that they know their limits, and don't push beyond them. There's no shame attached to these little defeats. Blue and Celeste understand that turning back is just as good as forging ahead; it's the journey, not the destination, that is important to them. "Don't push beyond your limits" seems to be the first rule of dog survival.

I had to go halfway around the world to the Buddhist kingdom of Bhutan to learn this same rule myself. Bhutan, which borders on India and Nepal, is a mostly mountainous country, and this particular trek was a constant up and down of rocky switchbacks alternating with mud-soaked valleys.

I was trekking with three close friends. We had expected to be totally alone in the wilderness, but much to our disgust seventeen men and women from the Seattle Mountaineering Club were hiking a parallel route to ours for the first five days of the trek. I jokingly told the Mountaineers that we four were members of the San Rafael Scrabble Club, so they would be properly humiliated if a bunch of nerds passed them along the trail. But there was no chance of that actually happening—the Mountaineers were some serious hikers. With their overstuffed day packs and mud-soaked gaiters, they left us far behind every morning. Since we always chose to take a very, very late lunch, however, we sometimes caught up with them having their group meal by the side of the river. As the tortoise momentarily passed the hare, I always made sure to let them overhear a few loudly-uttered, surefire scrabble words like *Armageddon*, and *kine*, and *rhinoplasty*, just to rub it in.

One of the members of the Seattle group whom I met on the trail was an experienced international mountain climber. Unfortunately, he had undergone knee replacement surgery just three months before, and his other knee was going to need surgery soon as well, so he had to limp along on two walking poles over all this rough terrain. He always lingered far behind his group, and even our motley crew was able to pass him on the trail.

Because of his twin walking poles, our guides called him "The Stick Man." One night The Stick Man still hadn't reached camp by ten o'clock, and his guides sent a horseman back for him. He refused to get on the horse and eventually hobbled into camp on his own power, well after midnight. That kind of macho behavior left the four of us shaking our heads in amazement.

But we four soon had a macho decision of our own to make. We were camped at Johmalari Base Camp, 14,000 feet up, at the base of a spectacular, snow-covered mountain that towered over the valley. Our original plan was to continue from there over two 17,000-foot passes, but Richard's hip was out of joint, one of Ken's knees was hurting, and Michael was unable to sleep at the high altitudes. Michael, who usually had the strength of a bull, was so weakened from lack of sleep that he could barely carry his daypack. I had hurt my back in a training hike the previous month, and although I thankfully hadn't reinjured it, I had definitely been punishing myself just to get this far. So the question was, do we push on, or do we turn back?

We all wanted desperately to continue on, but we knew that this was our last chance to turn back. No one wanted to pull the plug on the trek, but it was now or never. So we decided that it was time for a serious council, where we all promised to tell the truth.

As soon as we began to voice our concerns out loud, we realized there was no way we could go forward. It was immediately apparent that at that moment the four of us were better suited for a trip to the emergency room than an assault on a mountain pass. Ken's knee was the "identified patient" (the trail ahead would get steeper and steeper and would wreak havoc on his knees), but in truth each of us had his own compelling physical reason not to forge ahead. I was disappointed (as we all were) and also somewhat relieved. There was no way to deny that we had reached our physical limits. There was no choice but to turn back and to remember once again that the journey is more important than the destination.

I had picked the right country to learn this first rule of dog survival because Bhutan is probably the most dog-friendly nation in the world. When we emerged from the wilderness a week later, we saw dogs everywhere we went. Packs of dogs ran free in the capital city of Thimpu, and the guidebook warned us to wear earplugs at night because of the constant barking and howling in the streets. Our guide Wangchuk explained to us that in the Bhutanese Buddhist cosmology, one is reincarnated as a dog in the lifetime right before one comes back as a human being. Everyone believed that all the dogs in Bhutan were soon to become people. That's why the Bhutanese were so kind, loving, and respectful to their dogs.

It was clear to me that in honoring my doglike limits I was being kind, loving, and respectful to myself as well. There was no shame in turning back.

"I love my master;
Thus I perfume myself with
This long-rotten squirrel."

—Author Unknown

DOGS LIKE TREATS

Dogs do like treats. Their treats, however, don't necessarily involve tidbits of food from a box or table scraps. To a dog almost anything can be a treat. Dogs even find treats in those things that we humans think are truly disgusting.

Blue, my golden retriever, loves to "perfume" herself with rotten squirrels, dead fish, cow poop, and other unidentifiable matter that she can invariably locate with her built-in radar for the revolting. I used to believe that this attraction for the truly disgusting was a breed-specific trait since my standard poodle would never allow her paws to come into contact with filth. While Blue would—with obvious glee—dive in and then roll about in dirty, rancid water, Celeste would stand by and watch with obvious disdain. Her look of arrogance said, "What a classless pig!" That was before I discovered her favorite treat—"kitty nuggets."

Often, before my wife and I are ready for bed, Celeste decides that we should retire. She indicates her decision by getting up, stretching, and then walking to the bedroom door. Standing at the bedroom door, she looks back at us with a face that clearly says, "Time for bed, everyone!" Like the good companions that we are, we stop what we are doing, turn out the lights, and head for the sack.

This routine was played out numerous times before I realized that this pristine poodle's apparent readiness for bed was really a gigantic ruse to cover her attraction to the truly defiled. One night, soon after going to sleep, I awoke to a sound in the kitchen. I discovered that every night after we were all in bed and asleep, Celeste had been sneaking back into the kitchen to check the cat litter box for any leftover tootsie rolls. She absolutely loved her little feline fecal fiestas! I understood then that even poodles have an attraction for treats that I find profane and revolting.

Dogs are always on the lookout for treats in life. While cat poop might be a special treat to my poodle, she doesn't turn down liver pate or go on a hunger strike when denied those little kitty treats. She just looks for the next best treat that life has to offer. In fact, to my dogs, life is just a treat waiting to happen. I think that too often we humans have difficulty seeing life as a treat. We are far too likely to view life as a trick with a few treats scattered here and there to be enjoyed after we have paid our dues.

The poet Rilke wrote, "life has a rhythm of sorrow for all of us." As I often tell my lecture audiences, we were brought into the world against our will. Once we get here we soon discover that we will be taken from the world against our will. This alone is enough to engender a bit of cosmic bitterness in all of us! Just coming to grips with our own mortality may be enough sorrow for any one person to handle. However, we can be certain that will not be our only "rhythm of sorrow." Without a doubt, life for all of us will be filled with many stings from the universe.

Sometimes we must face major difficulties in our lives, like broken hearts, betrayals, failed relationships, major illness, and the loss of loved ones. At other times the difficulties will be just part of the everyday trouble of living life in the twenty-first century, like traffic jams, bad drivers, rude people, thoughtless friends, difficult bosses, or investments gone bad.

I am convinced that the quality of our lives will be determined to a great extent by how well we are able to enjoy the positive aspects in our lives—to look at life as a treat. Our happiness will also be shaped by how well we are able to accept and move on from the tricks that will necessarily make up a portion of our lives.

My old uncle Joe was one of the first people who taught me that life could be lived as a treat. He was a yardman by profession and never really had much success in life, at least when viewed from the perspective that most people have about success. By the usual standards in this country, he was a "poor" man.

Time and again when I was a young boy, we would be together just enjoying the very simple treats that life had to offer—a slow walk through the park, sitting silently on the front porch swing listening to the sound of crickets on a summer night, or perhaps enjoying a single-dip cone from Mr. Murray's corner drugstore. In those moments Uncle Joe had a favorite saying that he almost invariably uttered, "I wonder what the poor people are doing now?"

The irony of his words was never lost on me. He was telling me that we were not poor, regardless of our material possessions. He was letting me know that we are wealthy when we can enjoy the treats that life has to offer, and those treats are everywhere. No matter what our material circumstances, we never have to be poor. We can always perfume ourselves with the pure oils of a life lived well.

*"Today I sniffed
Many dogs' behinds. I celebrate
By kissing your face."*

—AUTHOR UNKNOWN

DOGS
LICK THEIR
PROBLEMS

I remember hearing when I was a boy that dogs have cleaner mouths than humans. I have been unable, over the years, to verify this claim. I must admit that I have been more than a little slovenly in my research on this issue because the truth is, I don't think I want to know.

I've always very much enjoyed the sloppy, carefree, and slurpy kisses that my dogs so willingly dole out. I'm not too eager to discover the truth about the bacterial cornucopia that must be going on inside my dogs' mouths.

Common sense tells me that a dog's tongue has got to be one of the foulest locations on planet earth. I asked my vet about my childhood belief about a dog's mouth, and he didn't give me a definitive answer. He did mention, however, that I should keep in mind that a dog's tongue serves as both a washcloth and toilet paper.

My dogs have no reservations about licking things that most humans would not consider touching with the most extreme end of their big toe, much less inviting them joyfully into their mouths. I will not, dear reader, upset your sensibilities and disgust you with the whole revolting list of things I have personally seen my dogs lick. If I did, however, this long list would necessarily include only those things I could identify. I am confident that the tongue lashing that my dogs have provided to unidentifiable matter would be nearly as long.

This licking is not of the dainty, "I'll just check it out and see if I like it" variety, either. My dogs lick with a profound and nearly incessant stroke that would, I'm sure, disable my tongue for days. They achieve a Zenlike state of spellbound concentration. They are so absorbed in the activity of their tongues that they seem to be at one with the lick.

In a sense, I think it is this undivided focus that we need to learn from our dogs when it comes to "licking" our own problems. If we could go after our problems—even the nastiest ones—with this same kind of concentration, attention to detail, and dedication, then I know our difficulties with life's problems would be decreased.

One thing I have noticed is that when my dogs are licking, they are fully involved in licking. Then, when they are finished, they move on to other things. I have noticed that too often, instead of licking our problems, we let them eat away at us. We let our problems work on us even when we aren't working on them. This leads to chronic misery and no resolution.

Part of the difficulty is that we don't focus clearly enough on the problem to fully understand it. Licking is a very intimate activity. If we want to lick our problems, then we need to get intimate with them. I know it is sometimes difficult to get close and friendly with our problems; yet, there is no way that we can see our way to a solution if we can't fully understand the problem.

Albert Einstein once wrote, "Problems cannot be solved at the same level of awareness that created them." There is no better way to find a new level of awareness than by breaking free of our old perceptions, habits, and ideas. There is a good chance that these old ways of being are, in fact, contributing to our problems. When confronted by a seemingly insurmountable problem, we need to look deeply into the real heart of the issue with eyes that are fresh. This will keep us from getting stuck, and can help us to find a creative solution.

It will also free us to have more time to kiss the dog.

*"I have never met a man so ignorant that
I couldn't learn something from him."*

—GALILEO GALILEI

DOGS KNOW
THAT EVERY
REAR END HAS
SOME VALUABLE
INFORMATION

G roucho Marx once remarked that, "Outside of a dog, a book is probably man's best friend; inside of a dog, it's too dark to read." I suppose that Groucho was right, unless you happen—like my dogs—to do your reading with your nose. When I take the dogs to the dog park, you would think that they were reading the entire *Encyclopedia Britannica*. They simply can't get enough of sniffing and being sniffed. Every trip to the dog park is a full-blown sniff-o-rama. My dogs go around checking out the rear ends of every dog in the park, collecting—I'm sure—all sorts of useful information.

Of course, my dogs aren't the only ones sniffing around. At the dog park you will find a completely nondiscriminatory approach to information gathering. You will see a Welsh corgi straining on his tiptoes to get a good whiff of a Great Dane and a Doberman bending low to check out a dachshund. All the dogs are also excited, it appears, to hurry and check their email.

There are no cats at the dog park, of course, but around the house my dogs find the cats' rear ends of profound interest, as well. Dogs are simply always on the lookout for valuable information wherever they find it. We humans, on the other hand, tend to be very dualistic in our thinking. I don't know how many times I have heard someone say, "There are only two kinds of people in the world," followed by some dualistic assessment of all humankind. For example, I recently heard someone say that there are only dog people and cat people. Let me say from my own personal experience that this is decidedly untrue. I love cats. Obviously, I love dogs, as well. I am sure also that there are plenty of people (pity their poor souls) who love neither dogs nor cats.

The only dualistic assessment of human beings that I am really willing to accept is there are only two kinds of people:

those who say there are only two kinds of people and those who do not. Obviously, count me among the latter.

One of the problems with dualistic thinking is that it leads us too quickly to divide the world into those who are valuable to us in some way and those who are not. This thinking makes us believe there are some people from whom we can learn and those who have nothing to teach us. When we limit ourselves in this way, we cut ourselves off from many opportunities to learn and grow. Instead of seeing everyone as someone who could potentially provide us with valuable information that will help us to develop our full potential, we eliminate some people based upon the most arbitrary of judgments.

My uncle, who has an M.A. in religion from Yale and a Ph.D. in philosophy from Harvard, after retiring from his career as a university professor, worked as a school bus driver because that's what he wanted to do. How many people would see him, in his rumpled old clothes, driving his bus and believe that he had much to offer them? Another uncle did not have advanced degrees; however, he did get a degree in history before spending his entire life working as a yardman. He was surely among the most interesting people I have ever met.

The truth is that everyone has a story. Every person we meet has a story that can, in some way, inform us and help us as we live the story of our own lives. When we acknowledge this truth and begin to look at others as potential sources of valuable information, we open ourselves up to new possibilities in our lives. In reality, the people who are most different from us probably have the most to teach us. The more we surround ourselves with people who are the same as we are, who hold the same views, and who share the same values, the greater the likelihood that we will shrink as human beings rather than grow.

Many times I have heard people use the old saying, "birds of a feather flock together," as a justification for hanging out with people who share their own opinions and lifestyle. As a matter of fact, this is absolutely untrue. If you check the woods surrounding my house, you will find all sorts of different birds hanging out together. Some, like the mockingbirds, are even learning new songs from other kinds of birds.

I can assure you of this, as well. If given even half of an opportunity, my dogs would definitely sniff a bird's rear end, too.

"Still waters run deep."

—AUTHOR UNKNOWN

DOGS KNOW THERE IS A TIME FOR SITTING AND STAYING

The first two things that I always teach my dogs are "sit" and "stay." I can usually accomplish this bit of training in the very first fifteen-minute training session with a puppy. With a little patience and eight ounces of cheese even the slowest canine students are able to sit and hold a stay by the end of the second session.

What dogs can learn in a very brief time some people can't seem to learn in a whole lifetime—that sitting and staying is an important part of life. It seems, instead, that our lifestyles are all about busyness. We rush from place to place, always at double-time, never able to slow down and just stay put. I'm in a "Hurry, hurry, hurry," is our anthem, but we don't have time to stop and sing it.

"What are we running from?" and "What are we running to?" are important questions we rarely stop to ask. When we do ask them, we rarely sit still long enough to hear the answer from our deep, inner self. We only have time for the superficial, shallow answer, "It's because I have so much to do." Then, we are off and running again.

Blue's vet, Dr. Jim Ahumada, has a sign in his treatment room that reads, SIT! STAY! THE DOCTOR WILL BE RIGHT WITH YOU. When I commented one day about the sign he said, "Oh, the dogs don't need it. They have lots of patience. It's only the people. They are always in such a big rush. They are the ones who need to be reminded to slow down."

What exactly is the big rush? The Zen master, Thich Nhat Hanh, often says to his students, "Our final earthly destination is the cemetery. Why is everyone in such a hurry to get there?"

We all need time in our daily lives to allow our minds to sit still. This profound truth is a lesson that has been taught by the great spiritual teachers throughout history.

Just like with our dogs, sitting and staying is a habit that must be acquired. We have to train ourselves—first with short periods of quiet and calm and then later with longer ones—to let go of all the busyness and running around. We don't have to spend forty days in the wilderness to realize the benefits of solitude.

If we can learn to take just fifteen minutes a day for sitting and staying, then within just a couple of weeks we will already begin to see the benefits in our lives. We will be less anxious, more centered, and less likely to be upset by the inevitable difficulties that life puts in our path. Just fifteen minutes to stop doing, stop thinking, and stop planning may be all we need. When we can give ourselves these fifteen minutes a day to do nothing more than relax totally and enjoy our breathing, we will discover why this whole sitting and staying thing is not just something we should be teaching our dogs—it is something we should be teaching ourselves.

*"My dog is worried about the economy because
Alpo is up to ninety-nine cents a can.
That's almost seven dollars in dog money."*

—JOEL WEINSTEIN

DOGS DON'T
COMPLAIN ABOUT
THE MENU

A recent survey found that 66 percent of people with dogs say that they prepare special meals for them. I freely admit to being among that group. Celeste has some fairly bad food allergies, so I often cook a special meal for her. I really don't like for the other dogs to feel left out, so sometimes I whip up a two-cheese omelet to mix with the regular dry food for Blue and Mead while I am poaching codfish for Celeste.

All of my dogs show enormous gratitude for their food, even on those evenings when all of their food comes right out of a bag. They seem to know only three responses to the food that I give them—gratitude, colossal gratitude, and downright giddy gratitude. Never once have they shown anything like a hint of a complaint about the menu.

One thing that so often blocks our path to happiness is that so many of us have the habit of complaining. We don't complain just about the menu. We complain about the weather, the government, and the price of groceries. We complain about nearly everything, including people who complain too much.

Chronic complaining indicates that we are letting the conditions in our lives rule us. It is a sign that we feel powerless, fearful, and depressed about the circumstances of our lives. It is clear, however, that so much of our happiness is determined not so much by the circumstances in our lives but by the way that we interpret those circumstances. When we complain about the way things are, we choose to see ourselves as the victims of the situation rather than learning to reframe things in ways that can serve us.

The great Stoic philosopher Epictetus, wrote, "[People] are disturbed not by things, but the views they take of things." This is why the very same meal, for example, could inspire gratitude in one person and complaining in another. I am convinced that the practice of gratitude in our lives is much better for ensuring happiness than the practice of complaining. I often hear people say, "Practice makes perfect." However, in reality practice usually just makes things "permanent." Whatever we do habitually will become very powerful in permanently shaping our attitudes and behaviors.

Presently, somewhere in the neighborhood of thirty thousand people die of malnutrition in the world every day. Fifteen thousand of them are children. Rather than complaining about the menu, I think practicing gratitude for the great good fortune of having enough to eat puts us much more in touch with the reality of our situation.

I don't mention these statistics about starvation to make anyone feel guilty. I mention them because I believe that if we can learn to view our lives with a sense of gratitude, then we are far more likely to be happy than if we spend our time complaining.

Some years back, the Zen Master teacher, Thich Nhat Hanh, taught me that I could bring much happiness to my life if—when I think things are not going so well—I focus my attention on the question, "What's not wrong?" When I pay attention to what is not wrong, even when some other things are most definitely going badly, I can save myself from getting trapped in negative thinking.

Sure, there are plenty of times I don't feel like fixing breakfast for myself, much less cooking up a special meal for the dogs. But considering the alternatives, how can I be anything but grateful that there's always more than enough food around our household? I feel very lucky that I am able to prepare special food for the ones I love. I feel very fortunate that I have a family—including three wonderful dogs—that loves me. Once I get started with this list, I can go on and on. For when I really start to pay attention, it is easy to see that there is always so much that is not wrong.

*"There is no psychiatrist in the world
like a puppy licking your face."*
—BERN WILLIAMS

DOGS KNOW
THE ANTIDOTE TO
STRESS

Tax Day is generally considered to be one of the most stressful days of the year. That's why the San Francisco SPCA always stations itself on the steps of the main post office in San Francisco on the evening of April 15. The volunteers from the SPCA bring dogs from the shelter whose sole purpose is to be petted by harried taxpayers who are rushing to the post office at the last minute.

The delighted taxpayers report that when they stop to pet the dogs, the stress of the day seems to melt away. They are able to take a breath and realize that their tension-filled day has had a happy ending—they've successfully beaten the postmark deadline for their tax filings. Dogs invariably have that kind of calming effect on us. When we're stressed out, having physical contact with a dog is one of the best things we can do for ourselves.

Our dogs create a safe, calm, holding environment around themselves, as they silently communicate to us, "Don't worry, it's all going to be okay. In fact, it's already okay right now! What could be better than this?" And if we're lucky, they send us off to face the remainder of our day with a lick on the face and a wag of the tail.

Our dogs can help us keep the stressful days in perspective. When we're feeling stressed out, we get a tunnel vision that the whole world revolves around our race against a deadline. We tend to forget that there's a big world out there that has nothing to do with our immediate problems and by tomorrow all of today's upsets will probably be just distant memories. By tomorrow we'll have moved on to something entirely different to feel stressed out about!

This morning I was running late trying to leave the house, feeling all nervous and jumpy that I wouldn't get to an important meeting on time. Celeste and Blue spotted me heading to my car and came running over, each of them holding on to one end of their big overstuffed toy snake. They launched into an energetic tug-of-war in front of the car, growling ferociously at each other all the while, and there was nothing for me to do but laugh. A feeling of delight at their comic antics swept over me, and a wave of relaxation followed in its wake. I began by laughing at them, but soon I was laughing at myself for having made myself so uptight. It felt great to let all the unnecessary tension drain right out of me before I got behind the wheel.

Dogs show us that love is the antidote to stress. Our dogs can open our hearts during the times when we keep them the most tightly closed down. That's why every April 15 should be National Hang Out with a Dog Day.

"Know thyself."

—SOCRATES

DOGS KNOW
WHAT THEY ARE

For as long as I can remember, I have been deeply interested in the old question of nurture versus nature. Every time I just about convince myself that environmental factors—family rearing, cultural experiences, or peer relationships—are the most important things shaping our lives, someone will tell me an amazing story that points to heredity as the primary factor. I hear of twin boys separated at birth and sent to different families in different parts of the world who both later become gay jugglers with Ph.D.'s in computer science. Then I become confused all over again.

The majority of thinkers have concluded that who and what we are is the result of a balanced interplay between nature and nurture. I imagine the same thing must be true for dogs.

I once lived above the Plaza de San Fernando in the beautiful colonial city of Guanajuato in Mexico. The Plaza was not only my front yard but also a favored hangout for lots of people, a variety of dogs, and about a thousand or so pigeons. My first day in the house, I noticed several children having a jolly time chasing the pigeons. It was quite a game. The pigeons would simply lift off and then alight again a few yards away in another part of the Plaza. I noticed also that occasionally one of the neighborhood dogs in the Plaza would take a half-hearted run at the birds. Just as with the children, the pigeons would rise slightly above the dog's head and move to another part of the Plaza.

When I first took my dogs out, they made a mad dash for the pigeons, and the pigeons did their casual liftoff routine. Much to my surprise, Mead, who has remarkable jumping ability, leapt into the air and snagged a pigeon in flight. She very proudly brought the pigeon straight to me. I was mortified and screamed, "Drop!" Mead instantly dropped the somewhat dazed bird at my feet. As I was scolding Mead, the pigeon took flight again only to have Blue grab him out of the air and bring him over to me.

All the people in the Plaza were having a great time watching the free show. In my halting Spanish I tried to get out a few words of explanation for the behavior of my dogs, *"Las Perritas les gustan...."* It was at this point that I realized that my vocabulary didn't include *catch*. So, while I stuttered, one of the onlookers helped me by filling in *comer*. "No!" I yelled, *"No les gustan comerlas."* They didn't like to *EAT* the pigeons, but I was without the words to explain exactly what they did want to do with them.

So, I changed my tactic. I decided to tell the crowd that these were birddogs. However, what I said actually was, *"Ellas son perritas de palomas!"* The people in the Plaza howled with laughter. That's when I realized that I had just informed them that my dogs were "pigeon dogs." To make matters even worse, there was Mead again with yet another pigeon to deposit at my feet.

Once again, I scolded the dogs as I got them on to their leashes. The dogs looked at me with truly perplexed looks that seemed to say, "Hey, what's the problem? We *are* bird-dogs, you know?" They were right. After all, what they were doing was as natural as the first breath of a newborn baby. I have never trained or used my dogs for hunting. For that matter, I have never even once considered going hunting myself. Yet, I realized that my dogs were simply doing what nature had beautifully prepared them to do. Through years of selective breeding, my dogs had acquired the innate skill and desire to retrieve birds, hold them as gently as possible in their mouths, and bring them to their human companions.

I am certain that my dogs—through training—could be programmed to resist the natural urge to catch birds. I would not be the first, however, to suggest that there is a price to pay when we don't live in harmony with our nature. The Stoic philosopher Epictetus taught that true happiness comes only when we can realize which parts of us are free and which are bound by nature. He went on to say that we should change what we can and accept what we cannot change.

Epictetus's simple prescription for happiness is something I find helpful every single day. "We can never fail to be happy," he argued, "if we can learn to desire that things should be exactly as they are."

"There's a whole lotta shakin' goin' on."

—JERRY LEE LEWIS

DOGS SHAKE
OFF THEIR PESTS

I've always been attracted to that full-bodied shake that is near universal in dogs. I see it regularly because my golden retriever misses no opportunity—regardless of the weather—to leap into any body of water she sees. Ocean, swimming pool, mud puddle, it doesn't matter to her. She loves water wherever she finds it.

She emerges from her dip, runs to the nearest person she can find, and rapidly shakes off any pesky water that remains. Her shudder starts with a subtle turn of the head and shoulders and then rapidly accelerates the length of her entire body. This includes a masterful vibration of her heavily feathered tail.

Her shakes are not reserved just for getting rid of water. She goes into the same quivering routine after rolling in dirt, dead fish, horse poop, or to get rid of an annoying fly. Sometimes, I'm convinced, she just shakes for the fun of it. When she breaks into one of her full trembles, she makes Jerry Lee Lewis, Elvis Presley, and all their modern-day descendants look like shaker wannabees.

She also has the half-shake, the quarter-shake, and the subtler hip, ear, and nose quivers in her repertoire. She usually uses these less vigorous maneuvers to rid herself of the various itches and pests that occasion her life.

I guess I've always loved these shaking movements because it seems to me such a great image for how we can deal with the nagging little worries, anxieties, and problems that we encounter every day. But many times we just carry these pests around with us instead of shaking them off, putting them behind us, and getting on with our lives.

When I was a young man involved in sports, a minor injury on the field would always evoke a clap of the hands from the coach and the simple imperative, "Okay now, shake it off!" The idea was to "keep your head in the game" and not get stuck in self-pity, or you were certain to lose concentration on whatever challenge was coming up next.

Many of us are unable to shake off the little annoyances in our everyday lives. (In fact we often call these little annoyances "pet peeves," but I've never actually known my pets to have any such peeves!) What we may not realize is that these petty annoyances have a way of keeping us stuck in negativity and pessimism, which is certainly not the best way to move toward a life of happiness.

It's always helpful to remember that we have a choice of how we view the world. The next time you catch yourself worrying and obsessing about the minor pests in your own life, it might be useful to conjure up the image of a dog that has just emerged from a dip in the lake. Whatever it is that's bothering you, it's time to make a choice: "Okay now, just shake it off!"

*"Only the flow matters; live and let live,
love and let love."*

—D. H. LAWRENCE

DOGS GO WITH
THE FLOW

One of the most comical sights in the world is Blue and Celeste walking backward. The dogs are always ready to forge ahead and stick their noses into anything that looks interesting. But as soon as they run into something that makes them even remotely anxious, they immediately shift into reverse gear and back out as quickly as they can. Dogs steer clear of trouble.

According to the Theory of Flow, that's exactly what they should be doing. *Flow* is the word that we most commonly use to describe great athletes during a game where they can do no wrong. On the night when every shot drops into the basket, when the basket itself looks as big as an ocean to them, we say that the players are "in the zone" or "in the flow."

Flow is a state of being at ease with life, of feeling "on purpose," of being in harmony with the world, but it's not a state that needs to be restricted to athletic competition. Flow can be happening for anyone, doing anything, at any time. One of the reasons dogs are so happy is because they instinctively follow the rules of flow.

In his landmark book called *Flow*, Mihaly Csikszentmihalyi proposes that flow takes place in the area between boredom and anxiety. If you are too bored with what you are doing, you need to increase the challenge to yourself. If you are too anxious with your situation, you need to ratchet down the level of difficulty to something you can handle more comfortably. Then, magically, you find yourself in that special place where the level of challenge exactly meets the cutting edge of your level of ability. You begin to live in the exalted place called Flow.

Bernie DeKoven, who is one of the foremost interpreters of Csikszentmihalyi's work, explains it this way: Suppose you don't know how to swim. Obviously it would be too anxiety-producing for you to jump right into the deep end of the pool, so instead you wade around in the shallow end. But pretty soon just wading around is too boring, so you begin splashing a bit and running back and forth from side to side, and . . . hey, this is fun! You're in a state of flow.

This, however, doesn't last forever. After a short while, doing the same thing over and over becomes boring again, so your job is to increase the challenge. Maybe you start skirting the edge of the deep area, or you stick your head underwater, and eventually you even learn how to swim. Your quest for flow helps you learn increasingly more complex behaviors.

Asking yourself, "Am I in the flow?" is a wonderfully simple way to keep your everyday life in balance. Stay on the lookout for new things to try out. Forge ahead with a sense of canine curiosity.

If things get too scary, back off. If things get too easy, try something more difficult.

Stay in the flow.

*"There is no faith which has never been broken
except that of a truly faithful dog."*

—Konrad Lorenz

Dogs Are
Faithful

I am fairly certain that you will remember the story of Ulysses and his faithful dog, Argos, from your reading of Book XVII of the *Odyssey*. What? You don't remember your Homer? Okay, here's the scoop:

Argos represents the virtue of faithfulness that we find in our dogs and is likely the oldest dog you will find in literature, to boot. He was a wonderful dog that was unmatched as a hunter. When Ulysses left Ithaca to fight in the bloody Trojan Wars, the dog fell upon very hard times. No one looked after him, and Argos ended up totally ignored, ridden with fleas, and sleeping on piles of cow and mule dung.

Twenty long years later (making Argos at least 140 in dog years), Ulysses returned to Ithaca disguised as a beggar. Not a single person recognized Ulysses; however, as soon as Argos saw his old master, he first pricked his ears, then lowered them, and started wagging his tail. When Ulysses realized he had encountered his old faithful dog, he secretly brushed back a tear, fearing that an open show of emotion would lead to the discovery of his true identity.

Argos had apparently fulfilled his destiny by waiting faithfully for Ulysses to return. So, right after joyfully greeting his old master, Argos lay down and died. I ask you, who among us can compare our own faithfulness to that of Argos? Or, for that matter, who can match the faithfulness of most dogs? I can only assume that the classic dog name, Fido, is derived from a frequently noted dog trait, fidelity.

We most often use the word *unfaithful* in describing a marriage gone wrong. But these sexual betrayals are not the only kinds of betrayal in modern life. Clearly, we all experience unhappiness from the little betrayals that happen on a regular basis throughout our lives. Family members, friends, lovers, and colleagues all let us down on occasion. Perhaps just as frequent as betrayals by other people are those times where we betray ourselves. I doubt that I am the only one who is aware of how often this happens. I have let myself down by being unfaithful to my own values, dreams, and goals so many times that I have lost count.

As a result of these disappointing interactions with other people, it becomes difficult for us to have a "primal trust" in others. Interestingly enough, the philosopher George Santayana called this kind of trust—that allows us to truly count on other people despite our worry and doubt—"animal faith." I personally prefer, "dog faith."

Whenever we feel betrayed, it becomes more difficult to trust again. However, if we cannot give our full trust to other people, it is exceedingly difficult to find happiness. Whenever we are betrayed, it is our challenge to learn to be forgiving and be able to offer our trust once again.

Homer doesn't share the story of Argos and Ulysses from the perspective of the dog. I imagine it must have been very difficult for Argos to keep his dog faith for those twenty years. I suspect that the poor old dog must have felt deeply betrayed. One day he is the beloved dog of the prince, and the next day he finds himself—without explanation—on a dung heap. I am fairly certain that few of us, under the same conditions, could respond with a faithful, loving, forgiving wag of the tail. I am convinced, however, that it is a truly worthy goal.

"All knowledge, the totality of all questions and all answers is contained in the dog."

—FRANZ KAFKA

DOGS RUN FREE

"If dogs run free, why not me?" asks Bob Dylan in "New Morning." Dylan voices a longing that all of us overly socialized humans feel—to be free from the artificial constraints of living in a civilized society that can sometimes make us feel tied to a leash. It makes no difference whether we're living on top of each other in crowded apartment buildings in large cities or occasionally running into our neighbors at the small town post office. There is always an unspoken set of rules and cultural inhibitions that governs our everyday interactions with other people. But still . . . it is great to run free once in a while!

One of the reasons we are attracted to dogs is that they are so uninhibited and free. Dogs seem to play by their own set of rules, their own inner logic. They live in a parallel, but different, universe from ours—a universe that allows them a freedom of spirit and a passion for life that is hugely appealing to us. When dogs bark at the wind or howl in the night, it stirs something inside of us that wants to be expressed, too.

Dogs are a constant source of amusement for us because they pay no attention to our social conventions. They stick their noses where they don't belong, they jump up on the couch, they happily gobble up the food that falls under the table. Dogs rarely hold themselves back from anything. They don't share our inhibitions. Their emotions are close to the surface, and they let them out whenever they feel them.

Folk singer Peter Alsop always delights his listeners with an audience-participation version of the song, "I Wanna Be a Dog." What makes Peter's version of the song so much fun is that he encourages the audience to make dog sounds while he sings the verses. Peter sings, "Oh, I wanna have dog breath!" and asks the audience to pant along four times for the chorus ("Pant! Pant! Pant! Pant!"). "I wanna chase after cars . . ." ("Pant! Pant! Pant! Pant!"). Everyone in the audience immediately starts grinning at each other. Where else do you ever have permission to stick out your tongue and breathe loudly in public?

Suddenly, Peter stops singing and glares at someone in the front row, as he pretends to recognize their heavy breathing. "Hey, did you call my room last night?" he asks, pointing his finger accusingly, and everyone laughs along with him. The climax of the evening comes when Peter sings, "I want the moon to make me hooooooooooowl" and then encourages everyone to howl along with him. The voices get wilder and louder, as a primal energy engulfs the entire audience. They are caught up in the howling vortex, they howl passionately for a few minutes, and then Peter returns to the song:

> *"I wanna sleep on the ground!*
> *Being human these days is gettin' too crazy,*
> *I just wanna be a hound!"*

The audience leaps to their feet as the song ends and gives Peter an enthusisastic standing ovation. They are applauding not only Peter's performance, but their own as well. For a brief moment in time, they let themselves break loose from their usual social constraints, howling their freedom in a thundering canine chorus.

They throw off their self-imposed chains. They give themselves permission to run free. And they like the feeling.

*"If there are no dogs in heaven, then when I die
I want to go where they went."*

—WILL ROGERS

DOGS DON'T
CARE ABOUT
BREED

One of the most touching songs to come out of the Civil Rights Movement was known simply as "The Dog Song." The narrator of the song, a young black child, sings about how he cannot play with his neighbor's children because his family is black, and their family is white. But nothing can stop their dogs from playing together! The chorus of the song, "My dog loves your dog, and your dog loves my dog" paints a poignant portrait of the way relations between humans could be if only people could act more like their dogs.

Dogs don't choose their friends, associates, or lovers on the basis of breed, color, or culture. In fact, in all my experiences with dogs, I can remember only one case of a dog even taking notice of the breed of another dog. When we brought Blue home as a puppy, we already had Casey, a golden retriever, and Sweet Dreams, our big black standard poodle. Since Blue was a golden retriever, we somehow had it in our minds that she would quickly bond with Casey Bear. Casey had always shown such mothering instincts and, unlike Sweet Dreams, *aloof* was not in her canine vocabulary.

Much to our surprise, Sweet Dreams would not allow Casey to go anywhere near the pup. Anytime that Casey came near the eight-week-old Blue, Sweet Dreams gave a very decisive warning growl. Casey and Sweet Dreams had always been the best of friends, but until Blue outgrew her puppy stage, Sweet Dreams was the mother-in-charge, and she let Casey know it regularly.

Some seven years later, after both Casey and Sweet Dreams had died, my wife and I noticed an amazing thing. Whenever we were out with Blue and saw a standard poodle, she simply could not be controlled until we allowed her to go over and say hello to the poodle. Blue, who never showed the least bit of agitation about any other dogs, simply would not stop protesting until we allowed her to go meet every poodle she encountered. The color of the poodle didn't matter one bit—Blue always had the same response. As we expected, when Blue met Celeste it was love at first sight.

This experience convinced me that in some instinctual way that we humans don't understand, dogs do recognize differences in breed. However, the thought of responding negatively to another dog simply because of color, breed, or culture does not, apparently, enter their minds. Dogs treat other dogs as individuals and respond to them based upon that individuality.

Some years back, Blue was attacked and bitten by a Doberman. The next time that Blue was at the dog park there were several Dobermans there. Just like she did with every other dog at the park, Blue made friends with the Dobies whenever they came over. There was no hint that in her mind was a thought like, "Well, I better stay away from them, you know what those Dobermans are like!" Such narrow-mindedness and stereotyping is foreign to a dog's way of life. Unfortunately, it is very difficult to grow up in our culture without—oftentimes in very subtle ways—being filled with prejudices, unfairness, and intolerance.

Martin Luther King, Jr. had a vision for humanity—a vision that allowed us to be different and celebrate those differences, to accept difference as a good thing, and be able to live together in harmony. In his famous speech delivered on the steps of the Lincoln Memorial, he said in part, "I have a dream that one day . . . little black boys and black girls will be able to join hands with little white boys and white girls and walk together as sisters and brothers."

Once again, our dogs are way ahead of us.

"Please please me, oh yeah, like I please you."
—JOHN LENNON AND PAUL MCCARTNEY

DOGS AIM
TO PLEASE

The fact is that I could have written an entire book about the qualities of our canine friends without a chapter on the dreaded issue of dog poop, but why dodge the messy issues?

(By the way, this book was never intended to provide dog-training tips; however, this time I simply cannot resist. There is never a need to rub any dog's nose in their poop in order to housebreak them. I'm going to guess that if you are reading this book, then there is an excellent chance that you, yourself, have been potty trained. I'm going to go even further out on a limb and say that you probably accomplished this feat without having someone shove your face in a dirty diaper. One does not have to be familiar with Freud or other psychologists to realize that elimination of waste is a much more difficult psychological issue for humans than for dogs. So if we humans can figure it out with a little positive reinforcement, then our dogs can, too.)

Admittedly, people's attitude toward dog poop is a little-discussed but very complex social, moral, psychological, and cultural issue. In fact, I have not spent time in any culture where the sight of a hunched-up dog was a highly cherished cultural event. Dealing with the results is perhaps an even less celebrated problem.

Not long ago I read an essay by David Sedaris in which he told of being shown a photograph by his Paris neighbors in which Jodi Foster was walking on a beach carrying a small plastic bag. Assuming that Sedaris was an expert on all things American, the perplexed Parisians wanted to know what she was carrying in the bag. According to Sedaris, his friends simply could not fathom the fact that this movie star was walking down the beach with a bag of dog poop! In many cultures, scooping poop is about as unexpected as legs on a snake.

In my most recent stay in Mexico, for example, I was looked upon like I had some weird fecal fetish as I followed my dogs around with plastic sacks. My one attempt to explain the behavior to perplexed onlookers was a total disaster. I didn't know the verb *to pick*, so I thought I would just substitute *to take* when I was accounting for what I was doing. I confidently told my neighbors, *"Yo creo que es muy bueno tocar el popo."* My wife enjoyed several good laughs for the next few days after kindly explaining that I had not told them that I thought it was good to "take" the poop. I had actually said I thought it was very good to "touch" it! No wonder they looked at me so strangely.

In any case, there is an undeniable fact that there is a dog-poop problem descending upon us. Studies are showing that the disease-causing bacteria contained in dog waste are adding to water pollution problems around the world. Dogs are now thought to be third on the list of contributors of coliform bacteria in contaminated waters. Americans, for example, now have better than 75 million dogs as companions. You don't have to be a math wizard or an animal expert to know this adds up to an enormous pile of tribulations.

The solution, of course, is for all of us to follow the lead of Ms. Foster and take responsibility for our dogs at both ends. However, over 40 percent of Americans acknowledge that they don't pick up after their dogs and aren't about to start anytime soon. By the way, the number one and two water polluters are humans and wild birds. I don't think we are going to be able to get either wild birds or dogs to change their toilet habits anytime soon, so I think the answer lies with the featherless bipeds of the trio.

I am sure, however, that our dogs will help us out in any way that they can because, in general, dogs do aim—both literally and figuratively—to please. I've found this to be true even with their elimination habits. At home my dogs very quickly adjusted to the one area in the yard that I designated for that purpose. About once a week I go on "poop patrol" and find that the dogs have faithfully kept their business dealings inside that area.

When we run together I always tie plastic bags around their collars for the predictable call of nature during the run—theirs, not mine. The dogs know—without having been taught—that stepping off the trail a few feet in order to drop their load is the most pleasing thing to me and to other runners.

When I contrast the cooperative spirit of canines with most humans, it seems that—once again—we would do well to be more like our dogs. Based on my own informal surveys, about 75 percent of us can't even leave the toilet seat in a pleasing position for each other! More than 50 percent of us fail to replace the toilet paper when we have used the last of a roll. Of that group 95 percent believe that as long as there is one razor-thin sheet left, then a roll isn't really finished!

I guess I would do well to leave further discussion of toilet issues behind, for—at bottom—that is not really the point. The point is that, for our dogs, doing whatever they can to please us is a core issue in their lives. Think how different our own relationships could be if we focused as attentively on pleasing those that we love. With very little effort on our part, we could be giving a great deal of pleasure to other people.

My experience has taught me that giving pleasure to others is one of the surest routes to getting pleasure for myself in return. "Come here my sweet-breathed dogs! I want to kiss your face!"

"She is your friend, your partner, your defender, your dog. You are her life, her love, her leader. She will be yours, faithful and true, to the last beat of her heart."

—AUTHOR UNKNOWN

DOGS ARE LOYAL

The ancient Greek philosophers thought that loyalty was among the most important of virtues. To my mind, loyalty doesn't seem to be as admired these days. Oh, we may give lip service to the virtue of loyalty, but talking about loyalty and actually being loyal are far different things.

For example, today we find that a company's loyalty to its employees is very often seen to fade when times are not so good. No better example in the decline in loyalty can be found than in our beloved sports franchises. Teams have little or no allegiance to players, and players return the favor the first time they see a better deal.

However, it's not just professional athletes who prize free agency. Contemporary books giving financial advice tell us all to be "free agents." Their reasoning, of course, is that we tend to change jobs frequently these days, and our employers are not going to be loyal to us, so we—like they—should just be looking out for Number One.

It would be a real stretch to claim that our culture is characterized by loyalty to family nowadays. With divorce rates very high and "long, committed relationships" about as long and committed as the first real problems that emerge, we don't see much loyalty in this arena anymore. Many friendships go by the wayside every day because of a lack of loyalty. Loyalty is in high demand but in short supply.

The loyalty of dogs to humans, however, has been steadfast for thousands of years. Frankly, I don't see dogs getting into free agency anytime soon. It makes no difference if one is a king or a street person, a dog's devotion to his or her human companion is going to be . . . well, dogged. I have never been the friend of a dog who has—even once—demonstrated anything but the highest in fidelity.

To me, the classic example of canine loyalty was that of a collie who, in the 1930's, was the dedicated friend and coworker of a sheepherder in Fort Benton, Montana. One day, in 1936, the shepherd was taken ill and hospitalized. Loyal dog that he was, the collie waited patiently outside the hospital for his friend to recover. However, the universe had another idea. His friend died.

The family requested that the shepherd's body be shipped back east for burial. His faithful companion followed in the procession as the casket was taken from the hospital to the train station. The dog, who had let out with an occasional moan during the procession, was even more distressed when he was not allowed to board the train with the casket.

The dog, whose name at the time was not known by the townspeople of Fort Benton, came to be known as Old Shep. For nearly six long years, Old Shep, without fail, met every passenger train as it came into the station. Old Shep surveyed the passengers of each train as they unloaded, looking for his partner.

On January 12, 1942, Old Shep—who by this time was very old with fading eyesight and hearing—was struck and killed by the arriving 10:57 train. The employees of the Great Northern Railroad buried the old collie dog and placed a marker at his grave. On the fiftieth anniversary of the collie's death, the people of Fort Benton decided that Old Shep's loyalty and devotion deserved even greater recognition. So, they raised $100,000 and commissioned Montana's best-known sculptor to construct a fitting bronze tribute of Old Shep.

I believe that the best tribute that each of us can provide to our dogs (and to everyone we love) is to generate in our own lives the kind of loyalty that Old Shep and his brother and sister canines, through all these many years, have given to us. I know that we will discover that those old Greek philosophers were right when they said that virtue is its own reward.

"Dogs are our link to paradise."

—MILAN KUNDERA

DOGS FOLLOW
THEIR NOSES

I wish that I had a nickel for every time someone has passed me when I am out walking with my dogs and said, "Are you walking those dogs or are they walking you?" Almost always when I hear this remark, my dogs are leashed, so—in reality—I am walking them. I have a plan. I know which way we are going. I know how long we will be out on our walk. We are out "getting some exercise." The dogs are pretty much under my control.

My favorite walks with the dogs, however, are when they walk me. On these occasions they are off the leash. They are totally liberated. I just follow them. They take me where they want to go.

The dogs just follow their noses. They are at ease with a total openness to whatever life presents them. They are ready to respond instinctively to whatever happens. They are—in a sense—outside of time and space. Life for them is spontaneous and free. They move without a set of plans, commitments, deadlines, or worries. They have no agenda except to purely be. On these outings they are like young children because they can express most truly who they really are. They are in paradise.

It is true that they do things on these outings. They chase squirrels, investigate holes, pick up sticks to carry for a while, and they smell, smell, smell. However, all of this doing occurs within the context of simply being. They are not there to get these things done. On these walks their lives are as natural as rain.

This is in such contrast to how most of us live our lives. We almost always have a plan, an agenda, and some sort of deadline for getting things done. Unlike our dogs, whose doing is just a part of being, our being seems to occur solely within the framework of doing. During the course of a typical day, some of the most frequent questions we hear are, "What do you do?" "What are you doing?" "What are you going to do this afternoon?" and "What are you going to do after that?"

Somehow we have a great deal of difficulty just being. Our lives, it seems, become defined by what we do; therefore, we have become fixated with doing. Much of our doing is the "getting and spending" that Wordsworth bemoaned many years ago. However, even when we are not consumed with consuming, we must still always be doing something. I believe that all this busyness gives us an illusory sense of security and control.

My dogs don't need to take along a map, a jacket, a hat, and an umbrella when we go out for a walk. Obviously, we can't always live this way. Often we must make plans, and we have many important and not-so-important things that we must do. However, it's also essential to save some time for just being, without doing. If you can imagine a room filled with objects but no space between the objects, then you can clearly understand that such a room would be unlivable.

Setting aside some time in our lives to cultivate the art of doing nothing makes the rest of our life much more livable. When we can give ourselves some time each day to become deeply involved in doing nothing, we may be able to dwell—like our dogs—in a state of naturalness. If we can learn to do that, then we can sniff out a bit of paradise on earth.

"This is courage: to bear unflinchingly what heaven sends."

—Euripides

DOGS ARE
COURAGEOUS

Winston Churchill once said that courage is the most important of all the virtues. His thinking was that all other virtues were in some way dependent upon our courage. Being honest is often a courageous act. So too is being fair, and showing kindness. Even the practice of love requires courage, since whenever we love we need to take risks and make ourselves vulnerable.

Are my dogs courageous? Seeing Blue afraid of the vacuum cleaner, Sweet Dreams quivering at the top of a flight of stairs, or Celeste cowering at the sight of a toy balloon dog that looks like Goofy does not exactly evoke thoughts of dog valor. On the other hand, even the greatest human heroes are not always fearless. I'm fairly certain that even the most brave and daring among us have some Goofy-balloonlike "skeletons" in our closets. So, while dogs may have a few idiosyncratic fears, there is no denying that they are great models of courage.

Perhaps the most obvious examples come from the many thousands of dogs over the centuries that have gone to war. In America's wars, dogs with names like Stubby, Lucky, Chips, Nemo, and Rin have performed acts of courage in situations that would make most of us shake with fear. Among other things, they have attacked machine-gun nests, captured prisoners, and thrown themselves upon enemy soldiers in order to save lives and protect their human handlers.

My favorite story of dog heroism is that of Wolf, who was one of about four thousand dogs that served with American forces in Vietnam. Wolf was a scout dog who saved the life of his handler, Army Specialist 4, Charlie Cargo. While they were on patrol, Wolf sensed impending danger and bit Specialist Cargo's hand as the only way to keep him from stepping on a land mine booby trap. Charlie Cargo still carries a scar on his hand as a reminder of Wolf's heroics. As he found out, there are evidently exceptions to the old saw, "Don't bite the hand that feeds you."

There is, however, a tragically sad side to the stories of the courage of American war dogs. One dog, Chips, was given the Silver Star for his courage in the line of duty during World War II and the Purple Heart for the wounds he received while single-footedly attacking a machine gunners' pillbox and taking the gunner prisoner. When the Commander of the Order of Purple Hearts complained that giving medals to a dog was debasing to the humans who had received the award, Chips's medals were revoked. No U.S. war dog since has been officially decorated.

Regrettably, things went from bad to worse for American war dogs. When U.S. forces withdrew from Vietnam, the Pentagon declared that the dogs were to be classified as equipment of war. The Pentagon ordered that the dogs be abandoned in place in Vietnam. No one knows what became of these authentic American heroes.

In an essay about war dogs Richard Ben Cramer quotes former Vietnam dog handler Tom Mitchell of San Diego. "When we were sick, they would comfort us, and when we were injured, they protected us. They didn't care how much money we had or what color our skin was. Heck, they didn't even care if we were good soldiers. They loved us unconditionally. And we loved them. Still do." The former dog handlers of Vietnam share not only a deep devotion to these American dog heroes but also outrage about the way their dogs were ultimately treated.

This heartbreaking story demonstrates clearly that the virtues exhibited by these dogs—virtues like courage, love, compassion, and most especially loyalty—are not necessarily shared by the humans who, in the end, had control over their lives. Sometimes we humans bite the paws that feed us.

"Curiouser and curiouser."

—Lewis Carrol

Dogs Are Curious

Although we've all heard the saying "curiosity killed the cat," our feline friends are not the only ones around the household who are curious. Dogs are notoriously curious, too. When we're out for a walk, Blue and Celeste are constantly pushing their noses up close to get a sniff of whatever I've stopped to take a look at. Whereas I usually hike a straight line down the center of the path, the dogs are always dashing from side to side, checking out one exciting thing after another. A bug is crawling along? How interesting! There's animal poop on the trail? Quite fascinating! The dogs' continual curiosity certainly helps keep them in great physical shape—they run four miles along their zigzag path for every one of mine.

Although it's also important for us humans to be curious about the outside environment, the place in our lives where we truly need to be more curious lies in investigating our inner landscape. If we approach our inner life with an attitude of canine curiosity, we can better understand the truth of what is going on with us at any given moment.

The hallmark of canine curiosity is that everything seems interesting, and everything is worth investigating and checking out. That's a great way to approach our own emotional states as well. When I notice I'm feeling upset, the best thing I can do is to be curious about it. I don't get upset about the fact that I'm upset, I don't wish I were feeling different than I am—I just try to feel curious about it. And so I ask myself some simple questions, like, "This is interesting. I wonder why I'm feeling so upset about this. Have I ever felt like this before? Does it remind me of something else? I say I'm feeling hurt by this person, but where exactly in my body do I feel this hurt? What is it about this person that always rubs me the wrong way? Why do I feel bad about myself whenever she's around? What part of this interaction is her fault, and what part is mine?"

Whenever I get upset, I try to get curious about it and ask myself these kinds of questions. A few months ago, for example, Celeste's brother Sam was going to the groomer for a haircut. I thought he'd like some company, so I sent Celeste along to have a bath. I told the groomer that under no circumstances was she to cut any of Celeste's hair—just give her a bath.

When Celeste returned home, I was shocked to see that huge sections of the fur on her tail had been sliced off. The groomer explained that the tail was matted, and she thought it was unhealthy to leave it the way it was.

All I could see was that Celeste's beautiful, unique dreadlocked tail was gone, and in its place was what my wife jokingly called "a little rat's tail." I was enraged by the whole episode. I was furious with the groomer. I knew for sure that the groomer was way out of line for not following my instructions, but I also saw that my emotional reaction to what she had done was way over the top. So, finally, I got curious. What, I wondered, was I really so upset about?

That was easy. Celeste looked horrible. I felt protective of her, and the groomer had made her look ridiculous. The more I thought about it, though, the more I realized that my intense anger could not really be explained by such a superficial answer. Did I really care so much what complete strangers might think about my dog's appearance that it would send me into a blind rage?

By asking even more questions about the deeper causes of my feelings, I was finally able to realize that my anger at the groomer was all bound up with my own needs as a child—to fit in, to look good, to be accepted by the other kids. I wasn't afraid that Celeste was going to look stupid when we went out for a walk—I was afraid that *I* was going to look stupid!

When I saw that my angry feelings came from a part of me that was still afraid of looking bad in front of other people, my feelings of rage about the situation disappeared. Yes, I was still annoyed with the groomer, but that felt appropriate—after all, she had disobeyed my specific instructions. I would certainly never give her any more of my business. But my out-of-control anger was no longer there.

I also noticed that I felt just fine about taking Celeste out for a walk. So out we went.

Admittedly, our problems and issues are not as simple as most of those that our dogs have. However, the process of coping with both simple and complex psychological issues is quite the same. It's all about being curious. The process starts with an honest recognition of the problem, moves to thinking about the causes of the upset, achieves some understanding about what's really behind the problem, and, finally, does something that will transform the situation.

Are you curious about whether this will really work for you? That's a great first step!

LESSON 63

"Laugh and the world laughs with you.
Bark and you have no earthly idea
how humans will respond."

—Conversations with Dog

Dogs Laugh
Freely and
Wastefully

Most people acknowledge that dogs are very playful. Whenever I talk about dogs laughing, however, these same people object. "Dogs don't laugh," they say. For years my standard response has been, "Yes they do. It's just that dogs laugh with their tails. Dogs laugh thousands of times every day!"

Now it appears that dogs laugh with their tails and with their mouths, as well. Recent neurobiological research is supporting the claim that dogs, as well as chimps and some other animals (including rats, for goodness sake!) do, in fact, laugh. Dogs don't vocalize their laugh in the same chopped up exhalation sound of "ha ha ha" that we recognize as laughter. It appears, rather, that dogs make a breathy, panting sound when they laugh. When researchers play a recording of this sound to other dogs, the dogs immediately start running to find toys, playfully wrestle and paw their companions, and exhibit "play bows." Some dogs just start laughing right back at the recording.

A recent study found that the average adult laughs fewer than ten times a day. I'm sure that many of us know people who don't even laugh once a day. The same study found that preschool children laugh more than four hundred times a day. Surely children and dogs must be the World Champions of Laughter.

The truth is that we adult humans are killing ourselves with seriousness. There is a great deal of scientific evidence to support the idea that people who take themselves too seriously have a good chance of ending up seriously ill. We have all heard the old adage "laughter is the best medicine." Likely that phrase was intended to suggest that laughter is good for the soul. Recent research is discovering that laughter is very good for the body, as well.

When I was a young boy, my mother was very interested

in health foods. I remember one day when she was reading how healthy onions were for us. She wondered if the old saying that "an apple a day keeps the doctor away" might be modified to read "an onion a day keeps the doctor away."

I said, "Mother, an onion a day will keep EVERYBODY away!"

In reality, several good belly laughs a day likely will do more to ensure our good mental and physical health than either an apple or onion. I am convinced that extreme seriousness should be classified as a terminal illness. Too often we humans treat life with such gravity that you would think that we had actually discovered some evidence that supports the idea that life should be taken seriously. We are always obsessing about one thing or another.

Physicists are now telling us that the universe had her birthday 13,700,000,000 years ago. They are saying that the earth had her birthday somewhere between 4,000,000,000 and 5,000,000,000 years ago. My own birthday was somewhat more than fifty years ago. When I look at those numbers side by side, this thought occurs to me, "Maybe, just maybe, I'm not what this is all about. Maybe I shouldn't be taking myself so seriously."

No doubt all of us should be attending to the message that our dogs are giving us about life—Lighten up! In fact, both of my dogs are sitting and looking at me at this very moment. I think they may be laughing at me! They probably think I am being way too serious for sitting and writing when I could be outside laughing and playing.

"*Mankind's true moral test, its fundamental test . . .
consists of its attitude towards those who are at its
mercy: animals. And in this respect mankind has
suffered a fundamental debacle, a debacle so
fundamental that all others stem from it.*"

—MILAN KUNDERA

DOGS ARE
SENSITIVE

There is a story told about the poet and writer Robert Louis Stevenson, who once while out walking observed a man abusing a dog. Stevenson said to the man, "Stop beating that dog immediately!" The man replied, "How dare you, sir! This is my dog!" To which Stevenson said, "It is not your dog, sir! This is God's dog."

Like Stevenson, I don't believe that we own dogs any more than we own children or others who are in our care. I think it is our great good fortune that we have come to have guardianship over these wonderful creatures. Obviously, I believe that dogs have many magnificent qualities. One of the things I admire in them most is their remarkable capacity for sensitivity toward others—both human and nonhuman alike.

I have heard hundreds of stories from dog lovers that relate the ability of dogs to show kindness, compassion, and concern when they sense the needs of others. It isn't just that they have acute physical senses, which of course they do. Dogs have a great ability to smell and hear, but this alone does not account for their responsiveness to the needs of others. They feel deeply with their hearts and souls, as well. I will never be convinced otherwise for I have experienced it in my dogs.

My wife and I have noticed this gift even in the many street dogs that we saw on a daily basis when we lived in Mexico. These dogs—who had suffered so much because of the thoughtlessness and insensitivity of humans and who had every reason to become cold, hard, and indifferent—showed us that they had not lost their power to respond with love to humans.

On several occasions we saw men (and young boys eager to follow their example) brutally kick stray dogs. Even though the dogs were totally innocent of wrongdoing, they would receive the cruel blows without fighting back. Sometimes these vicious attacks came from men walking with their own beloved pet on a leash. In psychology we refer to this as a *disconnect.*

Of course, our failure to be good guardians and faithful keepers of our trusts and obligations is not limited to Mexico. The same "fundamental debacle" can be witnessed all over the world. Dogs have been man's best friend, but unfortunately man has not been always a best friend to the dog. In the United States alone, about four million dogs are killed each year. The problem of dog overpopulation is monumental. Currently in the U.S., more than seven puppies are born for every child that is born. Dogs are abandoned on the streets to starve or left at animal shelters in massive numbers. Of those left at shelters, better than 60 percent are not adopted and, therefore, ultimately put to death. It is a worldwide problem from which we need to rescue our friends.

If we could just learn to be as sensitive as dogs, then we could stop this kind of needless suffering. Of course, by becoming more sensitive to the suffering of one living being we will, I believe, become more sensitive to all living beings. Albert Schweitzer wrote, "By ethical conduct toward all creatures, we enter into a spiritual relationship with the universe."

In the end, I think this will make us happier. Every major world religion and spiritual tradition has within it some version of the Law of Karma. This is the idea that we reap what we sow, that the fruit of our actions will ripen. In short, this is the law that says, "What goes around comes around."

If this is true—and I believe it is—then a sure way for our own lives to be blessed is to practice the kind of sensitivity to others that—for some unknown but wonderful reason—is so characteristic of dogs. In an essay called "Healing," Wendell Berry wrote, "There is . . . the pride of thinking oneself without teachers. The teachers are everywhere. What is wanted is a learner." We need look no further for our teachers in sensitivity than the dogs of the world.

"To help life reach full development, the good person is a friend of all living things."
—ALBERT SCHWEITZER

DOGS ARE
COMPASSIONATE

Many early philosophers, most notably René Descartes, argued that nonhuman animals can't experience feelings or emotions. Even today, when one claims that animals experience sadness, love, joy, or behave with compassion, there is a good chance of being accused of "anthropomorphism"—attributing human characteristics to something not human. Many scientists and thinkers simply cannot accept the idea that a dog, for example, could really love a person, much less another animal.

I am given to wonder if Descartes ever spent much time actually hanging out with dogs. I wish that he were around today so that I could ask him to explain hundreds of incidents of which I am aware that clearly show that animals have feelings.

For example, I recently read a story by Stephanie Laland, which told of an act of compassion by a German shepherd. It seems that a man named Eldon Bisbee had lost his French poodle in a blinding snowstorm in New York City. Mr. Bisbee searched for hours for the lost dog. He finally gave up all hope and with great sadness returned to his home.

At three o'clock in the morning, a taxi driver appeared at Mr. Bisbee's door inquiring whether he had lost a poodle. Mr. Bisbee had a joyful reunion with his dog and then was told the story of his dog's remarkable rescue. The cabdriver had been driving through the storm when a German shepherd ran in front of his taxi and refused to move. The cabbie tried his best to get the dog to move out of his way; however, the dog only whined and ran off to the side, as if trying to communicate something important.

The driver understood that the shepherd was clearly begging him to follow, so he walked after the dog. The shepherd led him to the poodle lying nearly frozen in the snow. Apparently, the poodle had been injured by a snowplow. The taxi driver was able to get an address from the poodle's collar and the rest—as they say—is history.

So, this is my question: "What's up with that, Mr. Descartes?" I can give an answer faster than he can say, "I think, therefore, I am." That German shepherd had all sorts of feelings. Those feelings—concern, empathy, and distress—led the dog to perform an act of kindness and compassion.

In much less dramatic circumstances, I have seen my own dogs act compassionately time and again. For many years, I have taken my dogs to class with me. Blue has probably gone with me more than the others because it really seems to make her happy.

Invariably, she walks into the room and individually says hello to all my students. On most days, she then settles in for a nice nap. (Blue is the only one allowed to nap in my classes!) However, on many occasions she will forego her nap at the front of the room and instead go lie down next to one or another of the students. On these occasions there is no pattern to where she lies down. After many years of observation and comments from the students whom she chose to visit, I have come to a conclusion. Blue always lay down next to a student who I later found out wasn't feeling so good that day—either physically or emotionally. She was comforting them. She was showing compassion. Don't ask me how she knows they are hurting, but trust me, she knows.

Perhaps it is because dogs are so compassionate with us humans that they have the capacity for drawing compassion out of us toward them, as well. Willa Rothman remembers taking her dog Liza with her to a Fourth of July party. When the fireworks began, Liza got frightened and ran to the car. "We knew she wanted to get in the car to feel safe," recounts Willa, "but I brought her back out onto the patio and told her to calm down, that she'd be safe with us." But as the fireworks got louder and louder, Liza became more and more agitated, and finally she just bolted.

"We ran after her, and then we got in the car and drove

around calling her name for hours, but we just couldn't find her. Finally we gave up the search and went home. We had a horrible, sleepless night, until the phone rang at about two in the morning. It was the owner of a tavern way over in the next town, and he had Liza. Her paws were all bloody from having run all that way, but aside from that she was fine.

"Over the next couple of days, we heard stories about Liza from people who had spotted her on her run across the county. Apparently she ran right down the middle of Highway 9, which is the biggest road around here. People were yelling at her, and honking horns at her, but they couldn't get her to move over to the side of the road, where she would be safe. She must have been too terrified to think straight. Out in the middle of the road, running right on the yellow line, she was in danger of being hit by cars from both directions.

"A number of different people told us that at some point in her mad dash down the highway, some driver started cruising slowly down the middle of the road behind her, flashing his lights so that all the oncoming cars would see her. And he followed Liza for a couple of miles until she finally ran off the highway and into the parking lot of the tavern, where the tavern owner found her. Whoever that stranger was, he saved Liza's life that night."

The world is full of opportunities for all of us to demonstrate our compassion. I believe that when we learn to match the compassion shown by our canine companions—or for that matter, unknown German shepherds and anonymous drivers who encounter stray dogs on the road—then the world will be a far better place to live.

"There is a time to hold on and a time to let go."

—UNKNOWN

DOGS KNOW WHEN TO HOLD ON

On a beautiful May afternoon my wife and I took Blue, Celeste, and Mead for a nice long run and walk at the beach. They ran, played, and swam with great enthusiasm. I threw the stick and the ball far out into the ocean. Celeste, in her usual manner, followed after Blue and Mead, barking when she thought they were going too far out to retrieve. Mead turned her head from the huge breakers and unintentionally bodysurfed back toward us. Blue, with her characteristic devil-may-care, breakneck attitude, crashed straight forward into the waves.

It was a quite wonderful day at the beach for both us and the dogs. We had one heart-stopping moment when Celeste discovered a full-grown seal out of the water, far down the beach. She ran circles around the confused seal, and Blue and Mead went charging to join her, barking wildly. We were able to get them all on the leash before any harm could come to the seal or the dogs. At least, that's what we thought.

I noticed that Blue had blood coming from her left nostril. I assumed that she had taken a direct hit from a wave, so I shrugged it off. "She'll be fine," I assured my wife. Blue had always been the most focused, toughest, most athletic dog I had ever known. She had never been sick a single day of her life. She started running with me daily when she was just eight weeks old. She had once run forty miles with me and was still ready for more. During one of our runs together a car struck her. I thought surely she was dead, but she merely hopped back up, ignored her scrapes and cuts, and gave me one of her "let's get on with it" looks. This dog was invincible. At least, that's what we thought.

All summer long there were trips to the vet, trips to specialists, and test after test. All had been inconclusive. Virtually every possibility had been ruled out; however, the nose continued to bleed. Finally, the vet suggested an MRI. Near the end of the summer we were devastated to learn that Blue had a nasal tumor that was malignant and that surgery was not an option.

The only treatment option available was to have Blue undergo weeks of radiation treatment. There were no guarantees; however, our vet told us that she had seen dogs respond to the treatment and get another eighteen months to two years of quality life. I was worried about the side effects—the loss of hair, the possibility of blindness in one eye, the physical drain on her body caused by weeks of radiation three times per week.

Many people could not understand and were not very subtle about expressing their views to us. How could we spend thousands of dollars for treatment on a dog that is terminally ill? Why not just put her to sleep? What's the point?

I guess the only point was that throughout all our lives there will be times that we must let go; however, there are also times to hold on. In all sorts of situations in our lives—our work, our relationships, our dreams, and, yes, even in matters of life and death—there will be times to hold on and times to let go. Our challenge is to do all that we can to wisely determine which is which. Blue, for months now, has been showing me every day—even through her difficulties with this disease—she still wants to hold on.

She has lost hair, lost most of her vision in one eye, and her nose still bleeds with regularity; however, she still wants to take me for my run every day. She still wants to play. She still takes joy in the wonderful gift known as the life experience. So, we are holding on.

Blue is just two treatments short of completing the entire series of radiation treatments. She has willingly gone for each treatment and even has had an enthusiastic wag of her tail for the doctor each time that I drop her off. Today, when I took her for her treatment she stopped outside the door. I assured her that it was okay. She refused to go inside. I hugged her, and together we turned around and headed for the car. There is a time to hold on and a time to let go. Wisdom knows the difference.

"Near this spot are deposited the remains of one who possessed beauty without vanity, strength without ferocity, and all the virtues of man without his vices. This praise which would be unmeaning flattery if inscribed over human ashes, is but just tribute to the memory of Boatswain, a dog...."

—Lord Byron

Dogs Dance
with Life and
Death

Death where is thy sting . . . life where is my ball?" This seemed to be the way that she was thinking on the very last day of life for Mo's Better Blue (a.k.a. Blue, Bluebell, Bluzer van Duzer, Monkey, and Little Pumpkin). Blue never stopped living, right up until the very end of her life.

In the late hours of an August afternoon, on the day that Blue was diagnosed with an inoperable nasal carcinoma, my wife and I were crying and grieving in anticipation of our great loss. Blue appeared in the doorway with her tail wagging vigorously and with a ball in her mouth. She totally ignored the tiny drops of blood dripping from her left nostril and rolling down on her favorite ball. Her whole being said with her usual enthusiasm, "I'm not dead yet. Let's play!" This is how she lived her entire ten years.

In the early morning on the day that she died, we went for our daily morning walk and jog. Like all of us, she had her favorite habits and rituals. One such ritual was to reach the park and then instantly fall upon her back and wiggle and waggle joyfully, as she moaned with great delight. She could not be disturbed or distracted from her habitual morning greeting to the universe. Whenever I saw her rock and roll on her back in this way, I always imagined her engaged in a great cosmic dance. In a sense she was—through her joyful experience—grasping what is essential in life. She was experiencing the dynamic, vibrating, moving, dancing nature of the universe.

Her nasal tumor had become so bad that she had to make a choice between breathing and eating. She chose to breathe, so she had stopped eating. Our vet told us that once she stopped eating, we would want to help her avoid the painful deterioration of her body. We would need to mercifully let her go. So, on a cool January morning, my best friend died just as she had lived.

Blue's message in death was the same message that she had communicated to all that knew her throughout her life: "Celebrate your life every moment that you have. No event in life is too small to celebrate. Live fully. Love and laugh wastefully. Take pleasure in the little things. Play and roll on your back in the park. Forgive even if you cannot forget—grudges only make you an unhappy being. Don't bite when a growl will do." And, her final lesson that last day, "Make every day of your life a dance, even when death is your final partner."

Dogs seem to instinctually understand this lesson, but we must learn or perhaps relearn it. Several years ago, I was spending the last days with my mother as she struggled to die. She was suffering from cancer, and she spent those last few days moving in and out of consciousness, lucidity, pain, and peace. Near the end, her longtime friend, with whom she shared a passion for dancing and many evenings on the dance floor, came for a final visit. I thought that my mother might have slipped away into a coma, so when her friend asked if she could still speak to her, I said, "I'm not sure if she can hear you, but it certainly won't hurt to try." My mother's friend leaned close to her ear and said, "Let's go dancing." I was surprised when my mother—without opening her eyes— whispered, "Let me get my dancing shoes." Those were the last words that I ever heard her speak.

A week before she died, she informed me that she had donated her body for medical research. When they took her body, the medical school explained that eventually her remains would be cremated, and I could choose whether the ashes would then be returned to the family or buried at a memorial site in the garden of the medical school.

I must admit to a light moment when my mother's remains arrived by registered mail. They came during early December and one of my family members—thinking it was a holiday present—shook it to try to identify the contents and then placed it under the tree! Once the mistake was discovered, we removed my mother's ashes from under the tree;

however, for the next year her ashes spent time in various locations around the house—under the bed, in the closet, and on the mantel.

The next spring I purchased some bamboo plants. I planted the bamboo in my backyard and—with my hands—I mixed my mother's ashes with the soil. Often now when I sit in my backyard and the wind blows, I can see my mother, dancing in the breeze. I see stillness and movement, spirit and matter, consciousness and unconsciousness, the present moment and eternity; death all entwined with life. It is in those moments that I feel most whole.

Fortunately, we don't have to have a terminal illness to ask if we are dancing with life and death. We don't have to die in order to dance our lives. We can be passionate about life, and courageous enough to dance—like my dog Blue—in the face of death.

Photographer Credits

Beals, Sharon, © 2003:
    Dogs Listen Deeply (Even If They Don't Understand)
    Dogs Keep Hoping
    Dogs Don't Mind Being the Butt of a Joke
    Dogs Are Enthusiastic and Energetic
    Dogs Don't Need Designer Water—An Open Toilet Seat Will Do
    Dogs Are Easily Entertained
    Dogs Don't Just Roll Over for Anyone
    Dogs Don't Care About Dog Breath
    Dogs Go with the Flow
    Dogs Know When to Hold On

Butler, Susie:
    Dogs Know How to Love
    Dogs Are Compassionate
    Dogs Are Patient

Levin, Kim, © 2003:
    Dogs Adapt to Change
    Dogs Love the One They Are With

Luter, Krista:
    Dogs Are Loyal

Paez, Lee:
    Dogs Are Happy
    Dogs Show Their Love Openly
    Dogs Love to Play
    Dogs Are Good Company
    Dogs Celebrate, Celebrate, Celebrate
    Dogs Don't Bite When a Growl Will Do
    Dogs, Even Old Ones, Can Learn New Tricks
    Dogs Know How to Get Comfortable
    Dogs Are Good Judges of Character
    Dogs Turn Work Into Play
    Dogs Know Their Limits

Dogs Know There Is a Time for Sitting and Staying
Dogs Shake Off Their Pests
Dogs Don't Care About Breed
Dogs Follow Their Noses
Dogs Are Courageous
Dogs Are Curious
Dogs Are Sensitive

Pollock, John:
Dogs Dance with Life and Death

Tucker, Toni, © 2003:
Dogs Rejoice in the Small Pleasures
Dogs Know the Antidote to Stress
Dogs Look Beneath the Surface
Dogs Lick Their Problems
Dogs Run Free

Weinstein, Matt:
Dogs Travel Lightly